JUNKIES JUDGES & JAIL

To the great Beadle.
with thanks for all your
work for Charity.
with very best wishes
+ kindest regards.

Denise

JUNKIES JUDGES & JAIL

by

Stephen D Smith

First Published in Great Britain in 2000 by
Neville-Douglas Publishing Ltd,
Clumber Lodge, Hemingfield Road,
Wombwell, Barnsley S73 OLY

ACKNOWLEDGEMENTS

The Author wishes to acknowledge the following:

Julian Binney; James Brandon; Graham 'Bodger' Broom; Norman Collier; Colourbooks Ltd; Keith Copley; Neil Crossland; David Eastwood; Fred from Eagle Star; Lewis 'The Mad Scotsman' Frame; Tom 'The Hemingfield Fussilier' Furniss; Keith Gleeson; Christopher 'Goody' Good; David Green; Haworth Graphics; David 'Over The' Hill; Michael Jarvis; The Estate of Tim Johnson Deceased; Bobby Knutt; Peter Large: David 'Bader' Lidster; Andrew Lovell; John McGinty; Jeni Morton; Neville-Douglas Publishing Ltd; Tim 'Tenbelly' Norburn; Sean 'Pagey' Page; Lionel Parker; Len Pigott; Trevor Purdy; Rotherham Magistrates Court; David 'Money Bags' Selley; Jennifer M Smith; Rebecca Eve Smith; Max Tuouy; Stagewear Unlimited: Martin Ward; Steven Wilford, Wilford Smith Solicitors; and Albert

This book is dedicated
to the memory of my mother, father,
brother and sister-in-law

ETHEL SMITH

DOUGLAS SMITH

NEVILLE SMITH

HEATHER SMITH

No longer with us.

PREFACE

A lot of water has gone under the bridge since *Boozers Ballcocks & Bail* and *Plonkers Plaintiffs & Pleas.* I had a wonderful year with Charlie Williams preparing his biography and meeting some great showbusiness characters who contributed to the book.

Then there was my journey into enlightenment with the Medium and Clairvoyant Trisha, who taught me all about the beliefs of spiritualism in bringing that period to a close.

So many kind people asked me if there was to be another book in the comedy series that I decided to give it another go and *Junkies Judges & Jail* was born, with a reprieve for so many of the characters who found favour in the two other editions.

I sincerely hope the kindness shown to me will be rewarded with this book of memories from my life in what was once one of the great professions.

I thank most warmly my friends Big Goody, the Great Jarvis, Bodger Broom, Bader Lidster, the mad Scotsman, Jack and Albert et al for allowing me to enjoy the pleasure of their company and recount so may of the events in which they have played a part. I have changed the names of those of my clients who appear in these pages to protect their anonymity but all the stories are based on fact and I have tried to tell it as it is, flowery language and all.

This volume takes us up to 1988 and will introduce some lively new characters who I met along the way.

Stephen D Smith
Yorkshire, 2000

FOREWORD

I first encountered Smithy when he rang me, introduced himself and requested a Tribute from me to place alongside others in the biography of my pal Charlie Williams. I said it would be a pleasure, and my contribution was faxed to him within the hour. Impressed with the speed of my reply I was offered a gift of *'Boozers'* and *'Plonkers'*. Never having turned down 'owt for nowt' in my life, I accepted the offer.

I read *'Boozers'* whilst 30000 feet in the air on the Heathrow-Munich leg of a heavy flight schedule to meet up with a cruise ship, amongst the German executives in Armani suits and rimless spectacles. Dressed in shorts, T-shirt and flip-flops and my laughing tackle activated into a fit of hysterics, their scrutiny confirmed that I must have been released from a mental institution!

Reading Smithy's books makes one an eavesdropper into his memory banks, invoking emotions of sadness, joy, pity, anger and utter frustration. Thought of as a saint by the rags, tags, bobtails, innocents and sinners of Rotherham, he comes across as a bold character, a champion of lost causes, invariably triumphant due in his unfailing tenacity and uncanny skill as a lawyer.

Friends since our first meeting, we enjoy each other's company, make each other laugh and share a passion for the God Bacchus. I have great respect for a man who can drink more port and brandy that me, although my liver is grateful that we don't see more of each other!

Bobby Knutt

CONTENTS

Chapter One

Keith Gleeson's Cock

"A..L..B..E..R..T." I shouted, but to no avail. The wagon train had disappeared over the brow of a hill taking Jack and Madge Heptonstall and their kids on the way to a new world. For Jack it was the world of legitimate work: something he had never known before. For the family, it was a new area to explore and settle down in.

I stood for some time with a smile on my face. Little did I know that it wouldn't be long before I was to see them again but if I told you how it came about...........you'd never believe it..................!!

I walked back to the office with a heavy heart because the family upon whom I had largely based my practice had left the area, perhaps for good. It was not just the work that I was going to miss; it was the family itself and especially Albert. I smiled to myself, shrugged my shoulders and set off back to the office. It was before the era of the mobile phone and consequently I was not forewarned of the delights that I was to face upon my return.

My mind was occupied by thoughts of the Heptonstall family, which comprised Jack, Madge and the children, Horace, Boris, Morris and Venn, Cloris, Doris, Lorris, Tyrone and of course Albert himself.

During the journey I could not help remembering Albert's first visit to my office when he tried to spear the fish in the fish tank, but then neither would I forget his handshake, which sometimes left me with an extremely large globule of bubble-gum stuck to the palm of my hand. It was just his little joke! I remembered all the scrapes he used to get

1

himself into including the taking of a police car without consent, and having more than just peripheral involvement in a theft amounting to thousands of Cuban cigars. How could I ever forget Albert's brother Morris and the AA caravan, which he nicked from an unsuspecting patrolman? It was odd to find humour in such a sad occasion, but they had moved out and it was unlikely that I would see them again. I also thought it unlikely that I would take up their offer of hospitality to share a caravan for a night or two with Albert and some of his erstwhile brothers in the middle of a field in Northumberland, surrounded by scores of pigeons.

Then of course there was the watch. The pocket-watch that Albert had given to me as a farewell gift was already burning a hole in my pocket. The inscription on the watch was to poor old Frank whoever he was in recognition of twenty-five years service with British Rail and Albert had dumped it upon me. It was then that I realised that I could have unwittingly involved myself in a clear case of handling stolen goods and what would a court think to my story? I imagined my explanation to the jury:

"He was a very good client of mine and when he left he bought me a present. There is nothing wrong in that." I then considered the Prosecutor's cross-examination:

"Of course, you knew he was a thief didn't you......and you knew he had a propensity for stealing property......and you knew that all the family were unemployed and in receipt of benefits..........and of course how do you explain the fact that the watch was inscribed to a gentleman called Frank.............?" That was it! It was true...it was handling stolen goods, and even if I didn't know that it was bent when I accepted it I knew now.

My pleasant humour towards Albert and his family suddenly changed when I realised that the watch may well be the nemesis of my legal career. "How would a judge sentence me for handling a stolen watch?" I asked myself. "My God," I thought, "Pull yourself together, it's not stolen. They would never drop you in it in that way.....but would they?" And then my thoughts centred upon being struck-off followed by the nick and the dreaded wickerwork basket treatment from the perverted inmates.

My deliberations led me to throw the watch into the River Don on my way back to the office and with it went my concern and guilt. I suppose it was a knee-jerk reaction but the thought of some prosecutor placing a piece of steel between my shoulder blades was too much for me.

When I got back to the office I was greeted by the lovely but much harassed Tracey our long-suffering receptionist.

"Can I have a word with you Mr Smith?" she asked in the midst of a busy waiting room, which included a galaxy of characters reminiscent of those who stare out at visitors to the Rogues Gallery at Madame Tussaud's.

I smiled at the waiting clients with a knowing nod and looked for their reactions. Some of them smiled back, some of them grunted, but one of them was fast asleep and couldn't care less. On my way into the back room I spotted one young woman at the end of the queue with a cut eye and a lump on her cheek which looked like an orange. From what I could see the wound looked fairly fresh, although a bloodstained handkerchief partially hid her injury and her embarrassment.

I smiled at her and almost in automatic pilot mode I asked her,

"How are you, all right?"

Of course she wasn't all right, she had got a gash on her eye which needed stitches and a Jaffa on the side of her cheek which needed an ice-pack at the very least.

"What a stupid bloody question, you idiot," I thought to myself as Tracey slammed the door firmly shut behind her in readiness to give me my client list.

"We've got one drunk who's fast asleep and thinks he's in the dole office, a man who's had a pig stolen from his allotment and wants to kill the main suspect, and you've seen the lady with her face bashed in by her husband. He is sitting in a car opposite the office waiting for her to come out to do the other side of her face," said Tracey. I could not get a word in edgeways as she continued.

"We have two conveyancing clients as well but I've had to put them in the back tea-room out of the way because they were not very impressed with our visiting drunk. Mr & Mrs Haigh have just married and the drunk has asked Mr Haigh if he has come to the office with his mother. She was offended as you might expect."

Just then our exchange was disturbed by the sound of someone vomiting.

"Oh, flipping heck," or something similar, I thought to myself as the office junior ran in and interrupted our conversation.

"'E's been sick, 'e 'as, all over the waiting room floor, the dirty old sod."

I gazed at the ceiling for inspiration and then went outside and surveyed the defiled area near the door. The man had done his best to leave the room in time but not before he had left us with a quarter of his dinner and the remnants of about eight pints of lager.

The drunk was about to walk back into the office but I barred his way, because I have to admit, I was most annoyed.

"You're not coming back in here after what you've done," I said, ushering him outside. I did not wish to offend my other clients by referring to him as a filthy drunken vomiting bastard so I waited until I was out of earshot when my temper got the better of me.

"You filthy drunken vomiting bastard," I yelled at him, "Don't ever come back into my office again!"

"Look Mr Burtoft," said the drunk, "I don't expect to be treated like that."

I realised that he had gone into the wrong office because I was not Mr Burtoft - he was a solicitor with an office next door.

"You haven't even got the right bloody office," I said to him, trying to retain my composure.

As the man slid to the floor, I resisted the sudden urge to kick him firmly and squarely in the thorax and he ended up in the doorway of the office next door where I left him sleeping soundly and snoring like a pig.

We were doing our best to clean up the office when a representative of a local extremist religious cult came in looking for donations. He was bald, apart from sprigs of hair at the back of his head, which curled obtrusively down to his shoulder in the form of a small plait, and was wearing what appeared to be a loose fitting dress in bright orange whilst carrying a bell in one hand.

"Have you got anything I can take?" he asked.

His request caused me to look down at the pile of vomit and look back at him. He smiled a curious smile and so did I as if to say, "I know what you are thinking."

"Have I called at an inopportune time?" he continued, as I turned to see a solitary figure standing in the doorway, staring aggressively into the reception area – an attitude which brought a squeal of fear from the lady with the damaged eye as she ran from her seat into the back room. The figure entered the doorway and in a loud, gruff and fearsome tone he shouted,

"I want my wife, bring 'er out 'ere or I'll fetch 'er!"

He pushed his way past the Holy Man, who fell to one side. I had a decision to make. Did I bar his way and risk being assaulted, or let him go and do goodness knows what to his wife or do the chivalrous but possibly foolhardy thing and hit him with the office hammer which was conveniently placed in reception? As I was about to reach for the hammer the Holy Man sprang to his feet, grabbed the man by the neck and in one swift movement pushed the aggressor's arm up his back before anyone could speak. Then with an eerie calm he spoke out,

"Peace brother, we don't want to cause anyone any suffering do we?"

The man yelled in pain and demanded his release.

"Get off me, you bald-headed bastard before I smash your face in."

"I don't think you're in a position to do anything brother," said the Holy Man. "We can either talk about this sensibly or I am afraid you will have to wait here until the police come. It is a matter for you. You can either stand still now or I will walk you out of this office not to return, otherwise I will have to secure my grasp by increasing the tension upon your arm and your shoulder will be dislocated. I can assure you the pain will be intolerable."

After a few seconds the aggressor realised that he had lost. Tracey telephoned the police and within a very short time the Holy Man frog-marched the bully to the door and into the waiting arms of two burly police officers who took him away.

"I'll get you for this," shouted the bully.

"Peace brother," said the Holy Man, "but before you go would you like to make a contribution?"

Before he could answer and make some sort of contribution, he was dragged away by the police.

The entire reception gave the Holy Man a round of applause and he smiled.

"Where did you learn that tactic?" I asked in astonished admiration.

"The Paras," said the man. "I used to be in the army, until I found the light. Would you like a leaflet?"

I was too grateful to be rude, so I took a leaflet and pushed a five-pound note into his collection box.

"Bless you brother," said the Holy Man who waved his arms around demonstratively and rang the little bells on his fingers before marching out, as I turned to the rest of the people in reception, who were still looking on in bewilderment and announced,

"Er...he's a former para ....he's found the light." With that they gave him a round of applause.

"Well, I think a cup of tea for everyone might be the order of the day," I continued, "Please give your order to the receptionist and I'll be with you shortly. Thank you."

I walked into the back room as if nothing had happened to find Marilyn Hitchin cowering in one of the interview rooms.

"It's all right, he's gone now, the police have got him," I said to reassure her.

"Thank God," she said, "He's made my life a misery since he lost his job. He seems to think it's my fault."

"Well, the nearest one always gets the stick," I suggested. "Look, I think the best thing we can do is to see about getting you an injunction if he is causing you this sort of problem. Have you got anywhere to live?"

"Yes, I can go back to my parents, but they are elderly and I don't want him there causing trouble."

"I'll issue proceedings for an injunction straightaway, and we'll get you into court tomorrow morning. I suppose he caused your injury?" I asked as sympathetically as I could.

She hung her head as if in shame and nodded her agreement without speaking, looking relieved as I set about completing the paperwork. As I was writing, I glanced at her to encourage answers to the various questions I had to ask, and despite her injuries and dishevelled condition, I observed that she was an attractive woman of some forty years of age but I was staggered when she gave me her birth date, for I was ten years out in my assumption.

"So you are thirty years of age?" I asked.

"Yes, that's right," she said, "Although I feel a lot older," she commented almost attempting to placate my surprise.

I did not answer and continued to complete the form.

" I think I will have to go for a divorce," she said. "I cannot put up with this any longer."

"Well, my experience is that if it happens as frequently as it's happening to you, it won't get any better. You have got to make a decision sooner or later as to whether or not you are prepared to put up with that way of life," I announced firmly.

She nodded reluctantly and I noticed that her hands were shaking as I passed my pen for her to sign the Legal Aid forms.

I could not help wondering why she had put up with such conduct but fortunately there were no children, to be used as pawns in the game of chess called 'matrimonial proceedings'. Some people believe that when lawyers become involved in these disputes, settlements are delayed whilst they fight things out between themselves and my own experience confirms this belief. No one wins in such circumstances, proving that delays in settlement cost money.

I advised her as to the procedure which would be adopted at court and suggested that she might visit the hospital to have a medical check-up. I arranged for one of the secretaries to give her a lift and a quick telephone call to her parents ensured her transport home accompanied by a sympathetic ear to listen to the events of the day.

My next client was Jackie Hampton, who was angry at having received injunction papers, which had been issued against him by his estranged wife who alleged that she had been subjected to matrimonial violence.

"She's a complete git," said Jackie, "She has exaggerated everything in that Affidavit. It makes me out to be a right bastard."

I took the Affidavit and read out a catalogue of sinful allegations.

"According to this Jackie, you are a right bastard!" I exclaimed.

"You know me Steve, I'll fight anybody, but I don't knock the wife about. All right, I've given her the odd slap when she's deserved it, but that's normal i'nt it?"

I didn't answer but reached for my notebook to list Jackie's observations on the allegations made against him, which latter were supported by evidence making the case against him look impossible to defend.

He left complaining bitterly that that law was one-sided in favour of the woman and when I gave him my opinion he reacted by saying that he intended to represent himself when he would sort everyone out. Another satisfied customer I thought as he slammed the door.

"Peace brother," I said to myself and "I'll stay and do a bit of work then," I said sarcastically as he was leaving.

He did not reply, and I assumed he couldn't care less. I was right.

When my last client interview had finished, I trod the weary path up to my own room to find a large number of files on my desk with a corresponding number of letters representing the post of the day. I noted the usual missives, advertisements, requests for sponsorship and of course the letters from defendants in prison. Land Rover had written to say that their vehicle was the best 4 x 4 on sale and there was a letter from a Japanese firm which disagreed with them. The only letter of interest amongst the 'non-business letters' was a request from a Lincoln man for funds to enable him to climb Mount Kilimanjaro in a polar bear outfit to raise money for the disadvantaged in Peru. The thought of a polar bear at base camp in Tanzania raised an eyebrow, but somehow I could not quite see the connection with the disadvantaged in Peru.

The letters from the prison however were always the best and it was interesting to see that new inmates acquired the prison 'twang' within a very short time of their indoctrination into the custodial setting. I never quite understood how it came about, but certain catch phrases were the order of the day and like fleas they spread to the other inmates with remarkable rapidity. Phrases such as 'Hey man, I need some warmth in the lungs' was transcribed into 'Hello old chap, may I have one of your cigarettes please?' and 'Hey Captain, my head is in bits' meant 'You're my solicitor, can't you see that I despise being locked up and my incarceration is having a profound effect upon me', and sometimes I was promoted in rank with 'Hey, Colonel these four walls are doing my head in', which roughly translated meant 'I respect you as my solicitor, in the hope that you will accept that I am finding it extremely difficult to function in a custodial setting without access to women, cigarettes, drink and drugs'.

It was a source of amazement to me in the middle nineteen eighties, to see just how many defendants laid claim to neurological problems with such sayings as, 'It's in my 'ead, man' and 'My 'ead can't accept it man', and my 'ead's telling me one thing and the court's telling me another, so my 'ead is destroyed man'.

Perhaps it was the prison service who played mind games with their guests, but the system taught the prisoners to place as much pressure as possible on their legal and probation representatives in the belief that the added stress would make them perform better.

I had one letter from a regular of mine called Eric Wilkes which was particularly interesting. He had a gravel voice, growled as he spoke and was addicted to nicotine so that the one pound ninety-six pence a week he received from the prison for sewing mail bags provided only twenty 'roll-ups' per day and thin ones at that.

Eric was normally a 'sixty a day man' whose entire thought processes were geared towards tobacco; its systematic acquisition and subsequent consumption. He therefore treated our office, not as that of his solicitor, but more as a merchant and tobacco import company. His letter explained that it was an intolerable state of affairs and one which could not possibly be allowed to continue. He saw it as our duty to provide him with a postal order each week so that he could increase his consumption to a more acceptable level. In addition, he had little or no entertainment during the day and he thought that this could be alleviated by my sending him a radio and supply of batteries.

I received a number of odd requests over the years but one of the best was from a lad called Alan Oldroyd who had a proclivity for burgling vacuum cleaner component shops. For some reason which was never really satisfactorily explained to me he requested a parachute remnant! I still wonder what he wanted it for but have never received a satisfactory explanation.

I answered all my post regretting my inability to send Mr Wilkes his tobacco and a ghetto-blaster explaining that my finances were 'in bits' and my bank manager was 'doing my head in man'. I respectfully suggested that he approach his relatives, but was interested to receive his reply, in which he pointed out that he had no real relatives and the ones who laid claim to that honour were all 'twats'. I too was elevated to the domain of 'twatdom' by my failure to deal with his request to his satisfaction.

It was indeed an odd profession. You had to labour intensively at your studies to enter what was once a revered profession, bearing the responsibility of a client's liberty, only to be called 'a twat' because you wouldn't buy one miscreant a radio and some batteries!

I pondered upon the proposition and for the first time in my career the realisation had come upon me that I was not as happy as I had once thought, but I passed off the melancholia in the belief that a micawberistic attitude would be better and the following day I was proved right.

My spirits were lifted by the presence of the Honourable Sean Page, who had visited the Cross Keys in search of some meat and potato pie, good company and ten pints of Stones bitter. He never liked to overdo it at lunchtime. Uncharacteristically he was carrying a plastic shopping-bag which appeared to have a quill of some sort sticking out of the top and with my curiosity getting the better of me, I asked Pagey what treasures were hidden inside.

"Oh, it's a brace of pheasant old bean. Old Wagger caught one up the arse with the side by side so the Old Girl is going to shove them in the oven and we'll have pheasant for dinner." Pagey had this 'British Raj' sort of speech more suited to the forties and fifties.

"Who's going to pluck them?" I asked curiously.

"The Trouble and Strife, old bean. She's volunteered".

"Oh really," I said, "Does she know about it?"

"Not yet old man but she'll be all right - she's not a bad old thing," replied Pagey as he puffed on a large Cuban cigar.

I stood back for a while and surveyed the scene. There he was, blond hair but balding, six feet one inch tall and a baby but puffy face, expounding the virtues of pheasants which he described as being well-hung.

"They've got to be well-hung, don't you know," said Pagey authoritatively.

13

"Haven't we all!" replied Wilford, as he started his fifth pint.

We were disturbed by the sound of raucous laughter, which belonged undeniably to Louis Frame, the mad Scotsman. He had been telling the latest tap room joke to Tim Johnson, the then manager of the Bradford and Bingley Building Society in town, and when he saw us he repeated it.

"Hang on a minute," said Dave Eastwood, a local insurance broker, "I told you that joke on the phone an hour ago," he said disappointedly.

"Aye," said Framey, "And it's a good joke too!"

The round of drinks had grown to eleven pints a time. There was me and Wilf, Jarvis and Broomie, Pagey and Norburn, Framey and Tim Johnson and David Whitehead, a local insurance broker who was known affectionately as Bluto, something which amused Pagey substantially every time he used the reference, and the aforementioned Dave Eastwood. They were actually a first-class group of blokes, who were all hard working but enjoyed a good laugh and a good drink at lunchtime.

Another insurance broker called Andrew Lovell arrived with what could only be described as the worst possible timing. The first round of drinks had almost gone and when Andrew surveyed the scene he realised his appearance would cost him dearly.

"I suppose it's my round," said Lovell dispiritedly.

"Certainly is dear boy," said Page, "I'll have a pint of lager, a large brandy and twenty Benson and Hedges, oh and a bacon and egg sandwich wouldn't come amiss."

Poor old Lovell bought his round with great dignity and on checking his change reluctantly made the observation,

"I'll not bother with a sandwich.   I don't appear to have enough money."

"Poor old twot," said Pagey, "Let's have a whip-round and get Lovell a bag of crisps."

Pagey thought his observation hilarious as he observed Lovell sitting dispassionately on a barstool.   As the hilarity subsided, my all-round vision spotted a familiar face entering the pub.   I should say that dealing with criminal work can sometimes make you more aware of people around you and you learn the knack of three hundred and sixty-degree vision, enabling you to spot bandits and scroungers from all angles.

I was joined by a Mr Bumble-like figure, resplendent in blue shorts and a Manchester United football shirt with short sleeves, which exposed a variety of highly artistic tattoos on powerful arms.   His face was full with a dark 'Che Guevara' moustache, his hair was receding, he was wearing glasses and he spoke with a lisp.   It was a rather likeable client of mine with an ever-ready wit called Keith Gleeson who moved towards me in an almost secretive fashion as though he was anxious not to be overheard.   He looked all around as if conscious that some lurking force may be spying upon him, whilst beckoning me towards him with his head so that I should move closer to catch his whisper.   I had thoughts of some impending disaster for his approach implied there were grave and weighty matters to impart.

"'As tha got a minute?" asked Keith surreptitiously.

"Yes, of course Keith, what's…………."

"Now," he said, "In private like………just me and thee………..on our own……….just us together……."

We left the group and went to sit at a small table out of earshot of any other customers. I sat down, put my pint on the table and gazed at an extremely contemplative Keith Gleeson. He was worried, I could tell.

As I engaged him in conversation he drank furiously from the pint of beer on the table. The problem was that it was my pint of beer and Gleeson hadn't got a drink. As I watched my beverage disappear I broke the silence.

"That's my beer you've just drunk," I said accusingly.

"Oh, cheers old mate," said Keith and he began to explain his plight oblivious to what he had done.

"That bastard Trevor's nicked my cock!" exclaimed Keith bluntly.

"I beg your pardon?" I asked, taken aback watching Keith drink the remnants of my pint of beer.

"Yes," said Gleeson, "A beautiful cock an' all, one of the best looking parrots you've ever seen...........the bastard!"

Keith was an extremely forthright man but you did have to guess sometimes what he was getting at.

"Wait a minute, Keith," I said, "Let me see if I've got this right. You have a cock-bird parrot and Trevor has stolen it from you. Is that what you are saying to me?"

"Not really," said Keith, "We both own the cock."

"So he's not stolen your cock?" I queried.

"Well, he's stolen half my cock, because half of it was 'is and he's nicked my 'alf."

The picture was becoming a little clearer.

"Look Keith, let's talk about this over a pint of beer."

"Ah, good," said Keith, "I could murder a drink."

"Yes, I thought you might," I said, sarcastically looking at my empty glass.

16

He gazed at the container in front of him and smiled whilst I went to the bar and was accused of dropping out of the gathering to avoid my round but when all the orders were taken in I paid for ten pints of beer, two pints of lager, one brandy, a pasty and ten Woodbines. Gleeson had shouted the order for the cigarettes. I shook my head and returned to Gleeson's table, where after two large gulps Gleeson's beer had all but gone, so I moved my pint onto the next table out of harm's way and Gleeson's reach.

"Just what has gone off? What's the crack?" I asked, using a well-known Rotherham expression.

I thought by using this Rotherhamesque colloquial expression, Keith would seize the nettle and tell me his story.

"Tha sees I 'ave a hen bird and it was just old enough to be mated so Trevor came round to my 'ouse one day and told me that Esmeralda........., that's the name of my hen bird by the way, looked as though she needed a cock........."

I could not suppress a smile as Keith continued.

"..........'e knows a bit about cocks and so 'e said that because they were the same family of bird, we should breed with them. I know enough about it to know that if it had three or four eggs and they 'atched, when the birds are grown up a bit they would fetch about five 'undred quid each."

"Really, as much as that?" I asked, feigning interest.

"Oh aye," replied Keith, "There's big money in parrots. Anyway, you're supposed to leave the cock with the 'en after it's laid an egg and when the young 'un is born you're supposed to leave 'em there otherwise the 'en bird will fret."

"Hen bird will what?" I asked.

17

"Fret, tha' knows, get a bit upset like."

"Oh, I understand," I replied, knowing full well that I was lying.

"Well, what's happened, she 'ad three eggs, that meant one apiece

"That's two," I interjected.

"Aye, and one for grabs," he continued. "I said I'd like to keep it but Trevor wanted it, so we couldn't agree on 'ow to do it and there were no point me giving him 'alf an egg were there, so we fell out."

"What happened then?" I asked.

"Well, one day 'e came down to the aviary and just took the bloody thing away. When I got up next morning the 'en had pulled all its feathers out to show its upset."

"Why had it done that?" I asked sympathetically.

"'Cos it were in a fret and when they fret they pull their feathers out. It looks a reight mess."

"And what's its sort of mental state?" I asked, failing to find the proper words to describe its disposition.

"Oh, it just sits in its cage and shivers like," said Gleeson. "Tha would feel cold if tha were a parrot and somebody pulled all thy feathers out."

"I'm sure I would," I said considering the prospect.

Gleeson finished his pint and looked eagerly at mine.

"Anyway, I'm not going to interrupt yer afternoon with yer friends," said Keith who had already done so. "I can bring Esmeralda round to see yer if yer wish."

"All right Keith," I said, "I've got some time free about five o'clock this afternoon, bring her in and we'll have a look and see what we can do."

18

"Reight," said Keith. "I don't want to take the law into my own 'ands. The last thing I want to do is go round to 'is 'ouse and give 'im a bit of four by two."

"Yes, the last thing I want you to do is to go round to his house and give him a bit of four be two. You'll end up with a charge with a bit of GBH and end up living at Cross Bars Motel!"

Gleeson shrugged his shoulders and replied,

"But it's cruel. I wouldn't mind, but you shouldn't be cruel to defenceless animals."

Here was a man who was not averse to a punch-up if the necessity arose and he could hold his own with the best of them, but he had a genuine love and respect for animals and cruelty to them found no favour with him.

I told Keith that I would look into the case to see whether or not there was any form of action we could take, having agreed that he could bring Esmeralda into the office later that day, after which I promised I would speak to a friend of mine at the County Court office to establish what sort of Summons they could recommend in these circumstances.

As Keith moved to the doors to leave, he turned and looked at me squarely in the face and said,

"So far as I'm concerned, with that bastard Trevor, it's cock or else!" and then he left.

Wilf had overheard part of the conversation and only the deafest of the deaf could have missed the final broadside which caused great hilarity amongst our group.

"What the bloody 'ell was that about?" said Wilf.

"Oh, he's got a bit of a problem with a bird."

"Oh," said Wilf, "Bit of two-timing eh?"

"Yes, in a way," I replied, not wishing to go into detail.

"What she look like then?" asked Pagey.

"Who?" I asked.

"Esmeralda," said Pagey, "She sounds like a bit of a goer."

"She's African," I continued.

Pagey raised his eyebrows,

"Oh, I say," he said, "A foreigner eh?"

"Yes, and she's pulled all her feathers out."

Pagey nodded again before looking at me quizzically. "Wears a head-dress does she?" queried Pagey. I did not bother to elaborate on what I had said. We were at cross purposes.

I made my way back to the office and found a very large bag of parrot seed on the reception desk.

"Mr Gleeson's left it, he says he will pick it up in the car later. He didn't want to carry it home," said a rather confused Tracey.

"Well, don't eat all of it then, remember it's not ours and he wants it back," I replied as I collected my messages.

"Anything important happened Tracey?" I asked.

"No," she replied smiling, "Do you wish me to keep the bird seed in here or are you going to take it?"

"No, I'll let you look after it," I said returning her smile.

I left for my room in the certain knowledge that Tracey believed that I had suffered a mental breakdown and as I walked into the room I couldn't help thinking that so had she.

I spent the next ten minutes on the telephone with a friend from the County Court to thank him for his valuable assistance and he thanked me for giving him the best laugh he had had that week. We concluded that Keith could issue a summons in the County Court but because the value was only small he could actually represent himself. As Legal Aid would not be available I wrote out a full list of instructions in the hope that he might be prepared to deal with it himself and leave me out of the equation.

I had a mixed bag of appointments that afternoon, but the real prize was at five o'clock when Keith Gleeson returned to haunt me about his bloody bird.

Mid-way through the afternoon I felt the pangs of hunger and my four o'clock appointment not having turned up I decided to call at the off-licence across the way to pursue my so-called desire for healthy eating by buying a chocolate bar plus a six-pack with which to entertain my guest later that afternoon.   It would mean one can for me, two cans for Gleeson and three for Wilf, who would get very upset if he were not to figure in the benefits of the transaction.

I was day-dreaming as I walked back to the office, when the sound of a van horn seized my attention.   I looked to the side of the road and saw a white Luton van which was being driven by a young man I recognised as being Craig Twates, a likeable lad employed by his mother Ursula who carried on business under the trade name of 'U Twates'. Ursula who owned a small light haulage business which operated around the South Yorkshire area was a fearsome but honest woman and Craig was terrified of her.   The van pulled up abruptly and he engaged me in conversation, asking me to advise him in relation to a road accident which had occurred when he had accidentally bumped into another car at a traffic island whilst he was carrying out a delivery.

He was 'bricking it', to use his expression, (a condition more commonly known as diarrhoea), for he had to confess the damage to his mother, something which caused him much fear and trepidation.

21

I advised him that the accident would have to be reported to his insurance company, but apparently all company correspondence was dealt with by his mother and so he was left with no alternative but to tell her. In my view and on the basis of the old maxim 'if all else fails, tell the truth' he was finally disposed to admitting the crime to his mother, which promptly caused him to start 'bricking it' again. After our discussion he drove off rather dispiritedly in the direction of the family premises with the weight of the world upon his shoulders.

In this job you sometimes have to give people news which they will not like and the natural reaction is to blame the solicitor who is first in the firing line when the truth comes out, although some clients think that you can wave a magic wand to solve their problems at a stroke. Miracles sometimes happen, but most of the time they don't.

As Craig set off he pulled out in front of a lorry, causing it to brake heavily to avoid a collision and as his van passed me I noticed the name on the side which had been affixed by sticky letters. The correct title was 'U Twates' but someone had mischievously removed the 'e' and the 's' from the end of the name and when I read it I couldn't help thinking of Craig's predicament, after which I thought about mine. Graffiti experts in Rotherham had a strange sense of humour.

Later that day at about five in the afternoon Mr Gleeson arrived at the office carrying a large cage which appeared to have been draped with a portion of someone's curtains. He walked into my room, put the cage on my desk and as he unveiled the object he announced with pride,

"This is Esmeralda."

I was shocked to see a rather sickly-looking bird, which was completely bald of feathers apart from two or three tufts on the top of its head and looking as though it was being primed ready for the oven.   I couldn't think of anything to say except,

"Hello Esmeralda."

Esmeralda did not reply but Keith spoke up for her.

"She's not very happy," said Keith.

"I can see that," I said thoughtfully.   "It was a white parrot then?" I asked.

"It was," said Gleeson dejectedly, "but she's not now."

I explained to Keith that there would be an argument concerning the question of ownership, but if the court believed his version and we were able to prove that the bird was 'fretting', he was in with a chance of a Court Order being granted returning the bird for such time as was necessary.

I explained that it was unlikely that Legal Aid would be granted for his case, but if I prepared the Court pleadings it was a case which he could conduct himself.   He was not impressed with this suggestion so I had to lighten the conversation.

"Can it speak?" I asked inquisitively.

"Argh," said Gleeson, "But only one word."

"Really, what word is that?"

"Knackers!" replied Gleeson.

"I beg your pardon," I said in surprise.

"Knackers!" repeated Gleeson.

"Really," I answered.   "Who taught it to say that?"

"Our lass," replied Gleeson.   "It's her favourite word!"

For a moment my mind wandered into a possible scenario in the unlikely event that the local vicar should visit the

Gleeson household and we were present to record the event.

"Hello Esmeralda. How are you today?" the local vicar would ask.

"Knackers!" came the reply.

I wondered if Gleeson had realised what he had done.

The conversation soon returned to the question of court proceedings which was clearly uppermost in Keith's mind.

"Do you mean I'll 'ave to go to court on me own?" asked Gleeson despondently.

"Well, yes it does, but you can tell the story very well."

"Argh, but what if 'e has a solicitor with 'im? It's going to be a bit one-sided then?"

"I don't think he will be represented Keith. You can't get Legal Aid and neither will he."

Gleeson lowered his chin and thought for a moment before announcing,

"I'll see thee reight," said Gleeson, "I don't expect thee to do it for nowt."

I could not help thinking that the prospect of my representing the most unlikely bird fancier on earth in the County Court with other solicitors taking the mickey filled me full of dread. I have to admit that County Court law was not my strong point and all I needed was some smart-arsed Judge, who knew all about parrots, asking me questions I couldn't answer, and my life would be turned from moderate happiness into complete misery. Nevertheless, I felt sorry for poor old Gleeson bearing in mind that the bird meant a lot to him, and the fact that he was one of my most loyal clients. Once again I was faced with a case I didn't want, a Plaintiff who was likely to be inside for GBH, a Judge who was bound to be an expert on the topic of exotic birds and a parrot who could only shout the word 'knackers'. I had that feeling in the pit of my stomach which told me that all was not well.

After a quarter of an hour of bartering Gleeson left, having promised me a free parrot from the next brood and the choice of one of his snakes. I was sitting reflecting upon these grave and weighty matters when Wilf opened my door.

"Have you got any of that lager left?" he enquired.

There was one can left and my eyes moved to the right where it was standing. Wilf did the same and it was almost as if we were two gunfighters waiting to see who was quickest on the draw. Wilf won and strode out of my room majestically, having seized the can.

"You don't want to share it then?" I shouted.

"Sorry, I didn't hear you," said Wilf.

"That's all right," I said, "you'll not have heard we have just bought an office parrot will you?"

Wilf's door slammed firmly shut. I don't think he liked parrots.

I was disturbed by Tracey who was getting ready to leave.

"I'll lock up then," said Tracey. "Do you need me for anything else?"

"You don't know anything about parrots, Tracey do you?" I asked seriously.

"Don't be daft," she said. "I'll lock up then."

As she left I wondered what the reception area would look like with a large parrot cage in the corner, whose occupant repeatedly shouted 'knackers' at my visitors.

As I packed my things away I realised I could well have made a grave error of judgement.

Just before I left the office I reached into my coat pocket for my keys only to find a small jewellery box lodged in the mouth of a leather glove, and I immediately recognised it as the box which had carried the offending watch Albert had given to me earlier that day. I had been so busy disposing of the watch and my guilt that I completely forgot about the box.

I walked along the side of the canal to my car looking at the box when I saw a tiny slip of paper sticking out from the inside. Curiosity got the better of me and so I opened it to find a receipt from a second-hand jeweller with Albert's name endorsed upon it. It was bona fide and showed that Albert had indeed bought the watch and therefore it couldn't have been stolen. I looked up to the heavens but my tongue got the better of me and everyone's parentage came into question.

Chapter Two

Of all the Gin Joints in all the world
I had to be sent to Goole

Although the majority of my court work was in the immediate South Yorkshire area, I was asked to work in the 'foreign' courts from time to time. A foreign court is one other than in your hometown and whilst it is nice to work out of area occasionally, it can be a nightmare if you have to visit two courts on the same day. Solicitors who deal with these sorts of cases are always faced with the dilemma of which court to go to first since it is vital that you get on first to avoid being late for the other court and vice versa. Sometimes it works out beautifully and you can return to base just in time to get your cases called on before the inevitable bollocking for being late, but sometimes it doesn't. This is when you find out what stress is all about. The days are now gone where courts were quite happy to adjourn for half an hour for a cup of tea and a mid-morning chat whilst they wait for your grand entrance. The pressure is now upon us to deal with too many cases in too few courts with magistrates who quite understandably get irritated because of the ever increasing workload and the Lord Chancellor's predilection for statistics and a legal service who will work for nothing.

I have noticed during the thirty-plus years I have served in the legal profession that matters have got steadily worse owing to Legal Aid cutbacks, and solicitors are being asked to deal with more and more work to keep pace with an increase in overheads. Looking back I would say that by 1985 we were seeing the end of the best years of the legal profession, certainly so far as the Legal Aid practitioner was concerned.

Solicitors have been represented badly by their organisations such that we are not seen to be consumer friendly and latter day comments about the so-called 'fat cats' tend to push the population into believing that all solicitors fall into that category. Nothing could be further from the truth. Large firms with massive private practices do earn substantial sums and they would say it is consistent with the degree of difficulty responsibility and importance of the work they perform. The average run of the mill Legal Aid practitioner however does not aspire to such financial glory and fewer still attain it. He has to work extremely hard, be prepared to turn out at any time of the night, deal with all sorts of obnoxious characters, submit to harassment and bullying by certain of the judiciary without the right to answer back, and then fight for his fees at the end of the day. It is unfortunate that the public do not see how things really work but a week shadowing your average Legal Aid practitioner would be an eye-opener to say the very least.

And so it was in 1985 when I found myself considering the list for the following day with cases in Rotherham, Sheffield and Barnsley together with a very important drug case in Goole.

The cases in Sheffield and Barnsley could be sent to an agent, that is to say given to another solicitor who would act as my stand-in but the case in Goole was very serious and was likely to end up at the Crown Court. The two Defendants were in custody and wished to apply for bail and more importantly, one of them was a regular and in so far as loyalty extends to the criminal classes, he was loyal.

The quandary was which court should I attend first. The other problem was that it was a Friday and so far that week everything had gone extremely well, but experience told me that the bubble would have to burst sometime and Goole seemed like as good a place as any for it to happen.

I wandered up to the Cross Keys for a livener and quite by chance I bumped into Glenys Newton who was the mother of my male client who was appearing in the Goole Magistrates Court the following day. Her son, Danny Turner, was her oldest child by her first marriage and he had been charged with possessing heroin with intent to supply. His co-accused was his girlfriend/common-law wife Davina Chester. Danny was a regular and at thirty years of age he already had a number of convictions for drug related offences which were symptomatic of his need. Despite this tragedy Danny was quite a bright lad, having done well at school, but when he got to the age of seventeen opiates entered his life, bringing the side effects of dishonesty and an ever-increasing irrationality driven by the need to increase dosage when his flirtation turned to dependence.

My journey to Goole took about forty-five minutes and being early I found the court was closed so I decided to look around the town centre to see if there was a suitable site to enjoy a bacon sandwich as the best way to start the day. I'm not interested in the healthy form of grilling to reduce fat; the traditional frying with the bread dipped in the pan oozing cholesterol suits me down to the ground.

I found one such decent-looking coffee bar on the main street so I called in, ordered two bacon sandwiches and a drinking chocolate before being directed to a table and told that my order would be delivered, 'as soon as Eedie gets back from the lav'.

I was sitting opposite the counter studying the morning paper when three old ladies came in, ordered tea, and sat at a table opposite.   You could not help but overhear the conversation.

"Oh, she 'as suffered," said the fat lady.

"She 'as that," said the tall lady.

"No one worse," said the small lady.

"They were just like grapes," said the fat lady.

Then my sandwiches were delivered and I tucked in with the first bite, closing my eyes and sitting back in unconfined pleasure.

"'ave you seen them then?" asked the tall lady.

"I certainly 'ave, just like grapes as I've said."

I took another bite of the delicious sandwich.

"I don't think I'd like to see them," said the small lady.

"You'd get a shock," said the fat lady, "I've never seen anything like them, she couldn't walk a straight line."

"They say that tight belts and sitting on wet seats brings it on," said the small lady.

"Get away," said the tall lady, "I've got a tight belt but I've never 'ad them."

"It runs in the family, so they say," said the small lady.

"Well, it galloped in 'ers then," said the fat lady seriously, "Just like grapes they are, just like grapes."

I was just about to finish my first sandwich when one of the ladies looked across at me, smiled and pointed to the salt.   I walked the short distance between the two tables and handed over the plastic container for which she thanked me.

"Thank you very much young man, that's very nice of you."

She turned to lady number two and spoke.

"Very nice that, wasn't it Agnes?"

"What was that dear?" asked Agnes, "The grapes?"

"No, that young man across there," said number one.

"That young man across there?" said lady number two, "'as he got them as well?"

"No," said the fat lady, "He passed you the salt."

"Salt? No I don't think I want any of that dear. Anyway she wants to go and have that done."

"I don't think she'll do that, there's far too much pain. They 'ave to sit on a tyre for a month you know," said the fat lady.

"Well, 'ow does she go on when....you know....she 'as to ......you know?"

"Perish the thought," said the fat lady, "Ooh, she 'as suffered."

"Are we paying a call before we go?" asked the small lady. They all agreed, and they wandered off to 'use the facilities'. I had just about finished my bacon sandwich when they returned, waved to me and smiled, and then started to make for the door.

"Terrible pain," said the fat lady, "Terrible pain. She's got my sympathy, I'll tell you that."

"And mine," I thought to myself, "And mine."

I walked to the courthouse to find the door slightly ajar. It was 9.30 and a cleaner was busy at work sweeping the entrance.

"Can you tell me which way to go for the prisoners?" I asked politely.

"Next door, police station," she said abruptly, "They don't bring them round here until 9.45, the Clerk's most specific about that. He likes the general order of things, doesn't like to be messed about, likes to get on with it. Everything has it's place and it's all got to be in time, all got to be in order……..no messing about with him. There are those that don't like him, but I don't care really, I do my job and then go. Anyway, you'd better try the police station, I've got to get on, I can't spend my time standing here talking to you."

I was told that Goole was an unusual place but had not previously realised just how many unusual people lived there as I made my way to the police station where my two prisoners were brought into the interview room to see me.

First Danny and then Devina were shepherded in by a burly-looking policewoman who looked like a wrestler. She had an extremely deep voice, much deeper than mine, which boomed out as she spoke, whilst locking the door behind us. It seemed a little unnecessary as I couldn't imagine anyone trying to escape and getting past her but before I could greet them both they were locked in a seemingly endless embrace. There was nowhere for me to go so I just had to sit there and endure it.

"Excuse me," I said sympathetically, "Sorry to be a nuisance but do you think we could have a chat about these charges?"

They both laughed and sat down at the makeshift table opposite me.

"I might as well tell you from the start, these charges are serious. You've both got possession of Class A Heroin but more importantly you both have a charge of possession of Class A Heroin with intent to supply. There's a third charge of supplying someone called Sean Caxton, whoever he is and it's inevitable that these charges will go to Crown Court because I'm told they've collected about £1000 worth of Heroin from the house."

"Not guilty," said Danny, "Have you got any fags?" Devina made no reply until Danny looked at her and nudged her.

"It's all down to me," said Devina with a sigh. "I'm guilty and I'm admitting it."

I had that gut feeling that all was not well.

When I went into court, the Crown Prosecution Service representative was busily unloading three large black bags of files onto the bench in front of him and looking extremely harassed.

"Good morning, I'm Steve Smith, solicitor from Rotherham."

"Huh," came the reply.

"I'm sorry to bother you, but I wonder if I might ask you about the case of Chester and Newton."

"I haven't seen half of these files, which the police have just given to me, late, and I don't know how people can expect I should know anything about them. There's at least an hour's worth of reading material here. It's absolutely disgraceful."

"I'm very sorry about that. Would you like me to come back later?" I said, trying to appease him, sympathising with his problems.

"No, I suppose I'll have to deal with your query now," he said impatiently.

I resisted the urge to spoil my manners.

"Which case was it?" he snapped.

"Chester and Newton."

"Never heard of them.   Are you sure it's in the court?"

"Well, it's on your list," I said sarcastically.

"Well, I've not seen that file".

I looked down at the pile of files on his desk and spotted the Chester file under 'C', towards the beginning of the long row of files.

"This is the file I think," I said, attempting some form of conciliation between us.

The CPS man was slightly embarrassed which increased his annoyance even more.

"What is it you want to know?"

"Are you opposing bail, that's all?"

He fumbled through some of his papers before he spoke.

"This is supply of drugs according to this.   Of course I'll be opposing bail."

"But so far as the girl is concerned, she's no previous convictions at all."

"Well she will have when she gets convicted of this.   This court won't even try it, they'll send her to Crown Court."

"But that's not a reason for refusing bail."

"It is here," said the prosecutor   "The Court Clerk is Mr Croft and he's got a downer on drug cases."

"Well, it's not for the Court Clerk is it, it's for the Bench," I said as pleasantly as I could.

That's what you think...........No, I'm applying for custody for both of them.   The man's got a list of convictions a mile long."

"Well that I understand, but the girl......."

He interrupted me in mid-stream.

"I'm sorry, I've got to read the rest of my files now," and he turned away.

34

I could understand his annoyance, the pressure was on him with only ten minutes before the Bench came in and he would be bombarded with queries from defence solicitors from all angles and after all, I was a 'foreigner' from Rotherham. The old tradition of politeness to solicitors from 'out of town' had gone down with the Titanic.

We were joined by the Court Clerk, a tall grey-haired distinguished man of some sixty years or so, long overdue for retirement, who was even more snappy and aggressive than the prosecutor and viewed me with great suspicion. I had always been taught to smile when I met someone for the first time and to offer my hand to shake. Mr Croft was not impressed with either action and pretended he hadn't seen my hand as he fumbled with his papers.

"I have the case of Chester and Newton. It's a bail application and the prosecutor is asking that the case goes to Crown Court."

Mr Croft didn't reply and turned with his back towards me, putting some papers on the Magistrates bench behind him.

I decided I would try again.

"My name is Steve Smith, I'm a solicitor from Rotherham. I am coming to bother you with the case of Chester and Newton, which is a bail application."

"Yes, it will bother us, we've a horrendous list today."

"Well if it helps you, I've seen my clients and I know what the application is going to be and I am ready."

I looked around and saw that there were no other defence solicitors in the court room, so I thought this was my opportunity to get the case called on first.

"You're in the ten-thirty list," said Mr Croft.

"I beg your pardon?" I replied.

"You're in the ten-thirty list," he said forcefully, "It's five minutes to ten and I can't call you until ten-thirty. You'll have to wait for the other cases."

By this time my patience was beginning to be stretched somewhat.

"What other cases?"

"The other cases in the list."

I made an exaggerated look around the courtroom as if looking for other solicitors.

"I don't appear to see any other solicitors waiting to get on."

"Oh there will be," said the Court Clerk, and he turned away from me.

It had been a very bad start. I had a grumpy CPS man and a Court Clerk who seemed to resent my very presence.

I sat at the solicitor's bench and set out my papers in readiness. It was like the film *'High Noon'* when the tension builds up as people watch the clock, and Mr Croft was standing about anxiously in the hope that solicitors from the ten o'clock list would come into court and push me to the back of the queue.

The Magistrates walked into court at one minute past ten and bowed graciously; the Chairman was middle-aged with a pleasant face; the Magistrate on his left was a lady of similar age, with a tweed suit and pearls; the gentleman on his right was very smartly dressed in an extremely conservative suit, with white collar and tie. The Chairman was wearing a sports coat with a maroon shirt, which I thought totally inappropriate, but who was I to comment on dress code?

"Can we call the first case Mr Croft," said the Chairman.

"Will you look at your ten o'clock list sir?" said Mr Croft.

"Certainly," and the Chairman of the Magistrates looked across at me with a smile, expecting that I would be the first case to be called as I was the only solicitor present.

Mr Croft asked the usher if any of the solicitors for the ten o'clock list were ready and she hurried outside to return three or four minutes later to say that all the solicitors were busy in conference and were not immediately available.

"Have we any unrepresented defendants in the ten o'clock list?" asked Mr Croft.

By this time I was becoming a mite agitated at the rather disgraceful way that I was being treated, as the fact that I was from out of town should have caused the court to be courteous and call my case on first.   In the Rotherham court, where I spend most of my time, if we have a solicitor from a different area we always stand aside and give him precedence if at all possible.

The usher told the court that there was only one unrepresented defendant but he had decided to see a solicitor and so he was waiting for one to become free.

The Chairman spoke to me.

"Do you have a case?" said the Chairman.

"I do sir, I've already told Mr Croft.   My name is Steve Smith from Rotherham and I represent Chester and Newton," and then I couldn't resist, "But I am told they are in the ten-thirty list."

The Court Clerk turned to the Bench and confirmed what I said.

"Yes, they are in the ten-thirty list."

Then inexplicably, he turned and sat down in his chair, looking at the door as if waiting for a solicitor to appear.

"I wonder if Their Worships would like to retire until one of the other solicitors is ready?" asked Mr Croft.

I tutted furiously and shook my head before speaking to the Magistrates.

"Sir, with great respect to your learned Clerk, I am sitting here waiting, I have a case ready and although it's not in your ten o'clock list, rather than retire and do nothing would Your Worships kindly consider whether you could deal with my case?"

The Chairman spoke briefly to his two colleagues before announcing,

"I don't see why not Mr Smith. Could you call on that case Mr Croft?"

Mr Croft threw his pen to the desk, shook his head, and with great reluctance took my papers out of the ten-thirty pile of documents in front of him. I was troubled immediately by visions of Mr Croft putting the proverbial boot into me and my case, because he looked across at me and I could have sworn I saw the hint of a sneer.

The CPS man leaned across to me and whispered,

"You'll not get bail now."

I simply nodded and smiled whilst the defendants were brought into the dock and as Mr Croft read out the charges I studied them carefully.

On the one hand you had Danny, who was beginning to show the tell-tale signs of addiction, displaying a discoloration under his eyes, sniffing continuously and unable to remain still. Moreover he was sweating and appeared to be greatly agitated.

Davina was standing with her head bowed as if struck by shame. I hadn't realised but she was quite a pretty girl, who looked far younger than her years, so that as yet, the indications of drug taking had only just begun to rob her of her youth. She was actually a pleasant girl, not gifted with great intelligence, but generous of spirit and gentle by nature. She was from a very good home but her parents had disowned her in despair, owing to her dependence on drugs and the association with Danny.

She had a younger sister who was tipped for great things at school, having passed every examination that had been put before her and who was understandably the apple of her father's eye.

Davina had a wonderful relationship with her sister and whilst they still kept in contact they hadn't seen each other for over a year. This, an enduring family tragedy brought on solely by the scourge of drug-taking and about which she was powerless to do anything.

There was also the problem of her attachment to Danny. She was besotted with him; in a relationship where everyone can see it's a mistake except the girl concerned, and a relationship in which the harder her parents pushed, the further in Danny's direction she leaned. Her parents were honourable hard-working people: her father a bus driver, her mother an assistant with the school meals service, who together had built a nice home in a reasonable suburb of Rotherham where their daughters were well provided with education, home comforts and love. It was unfortunate that they had henceforth all become participants in an extension to a tragedy which now seemed inevitable.

"Did you say this is an application for bail?" asked Mr Croft"

I hadn't heard him as I was still thinking about Davina and her predicament.

"Are you listening Mr Smith?"

I was woken from my thoughts.

"Yes, it is a bail application Your Worships, for both defendants."

Mr Croft tutted again.

"I'm afraid it's a full bail application Your Worships, despite our list."

I resisted the temptation to empty the contents of my ink pen in his left ear and studied my notes.

The prosecutor opened with the facts which were that on various days the Drug Squad had kept observations outside the house where Davina and Danny lived and whose tenancy had been registered in Davina's name only, a point upon which the prosecutor made great play. Over the three days of observations no less than thirty people visited the house, five of whom were stopped and searched afterwards and were all found to be carrying small quantities of Heroin. They had all made statements to say that they had bought the Heroin from someone in the house, although they had been at pains not to name anyone. The following day the police had raided the house where they found a thousand pounds in cash, forty separate individual wraps of Heroin with a street value of four hundred pounds, and a set of weighing scales with a large number of small plastic bags.

The circumstances of the frequent visitors and the drug paraphernalia all indicated to the police that Chester and Newton were both mainstream suppliers, who accordingly were both arrested at the house with the items I've mentioned found on the living-room table. Whilst both defendants had denied the matters during interview, the evidence was sufficient to justify the charges.

Mr Croft nodded knowingly and it looked as though the decision had already been made.

I made a bail application, pinning my hopes for Danny on the fact that he was not the tenant of the house and whilst he was resident in the house at the time of these transactions he was not involved. For Davina, I pleaded that she was of good character and unlikely to re-offend if given help for her drug problem.

The difficulty was that the drugs obviously belonged to somebody and it had to be one of them, which fact rather limited the force of my bail application.

The Bench retired and were out for some time, until the bell rang and Mr Croft was asked to join them to give advice.

"That's the end of that then," said the CPS man, and sure enough within a matter of minutes Mr Croft returned with the Bench and a remand in custody for both defendants was announced.

I went to the cells afterwards to see them both to point out that they had the right to make a further bail application the following week, but that I wasn't too hopeful. Danny was annoyed but Davina said nothing.

The following week I attended Goole court and owing to circumstances beyond my control I was a little late, arriving at ten minutes past ten.

I went to the cells to see Davina and Danny and the police had kindly let them see each other prior to my arrival so that I joined them in one of the interview rooms where they were sitting holding hands. Danny was extremely pale and looked ill, but Davina looked quite well after the week's remand.

"I'm pleading guilty," said Davina, "It's my responsibility, Danny didn't know anything about it. It's my house anyway and he wasn't in a position to stop me."

She had blurted out this confession and then looked at Danny for some form of recognition. He smiled, squeezed her hand and then looked back at me.

"I'm not guilty Steve, you've heard what Davina says, we want to make a bail application for me and she's staying where she is."

"Not likely," I said, "If I'm applying for bail, I'm applying for you both."

"Yes, but you don't understand," said Danny, "She committed the offence, I'm innocent and if I apply I've got a much better chance. I've got to look after the house and there's a million things I've got to do, so I've got to get bail."

"What about Davina?" I asked.

"She's all right, she's going to get some bird and we think she'll have a better chance at getting weighed off if she's had some time on remand."

"Very convenient," I thought to myself, "Why on earth is this young girl allowing this to happen?"

"It's right Mr Smith," said Davina, "It's got to be this way."

It was pointless to try to discuss it further and so I went into the court. It was now twenty-five minutes past ten.

I was greeted with a nod from the CPS man who was in a much better frame of mind than the week before.

It was after ten-thirty when Mr Croft and the Bench reappeared from their deliberations and the defendant in the dock with whom they had been dealing was duly despatched to the Fine Office with a huge fine at which point Mr Croft saw me.

"I'm afraid you were in the ten o'clock list," he said smugly, "And it's now after ten-thirty, so the other cases have to have prominence.   If you'd been here on time you would have been called."

I rose to my feet and addressed the Bench not Mr Croft.

"Your Worships………..Your Worships……….I'm sorry I wasn't here at ten o'clock but there were difficulties on the M180."

"Yes, we heard the news," said the Magistrates reassuringly.

"I then had to go to the cells where my instructions were of such importance that I couldn't deal with them in just five minutes."

"We appreciate that," said the Chairman helpfully.

"I'm sorry sir….," interjected Mr Croft, "But we have now got to concentrate on the ten-thirty list."

The Chairman nodded, almost as if he'd been admonished by an over-bearing headmaster and sure enough another case was called on.

I was deep in thought until the facts of the next case were read out.   The defendant was a middle-aged man who had pleaded guilty to six charges of indecent exposure, or 'flashing' as it is more commonly known, and he had also asked for eighty other offences to be taken into consideration.

His solicitor leaned across to me as the Prosecutor was outlining the case and whispered,

"He's been bang at it," and indeed he had.

The defendant was a middle-aged man facing something of a personal crisis, which resulted in him behaving most inappropriately.   It seemed that he'd three previous appearances before court for doing the same thing, all within the past five years.

On the first appearance he was bound over to keep the peace and in his second he was given a conditional discharge for six months. The third appearance resulted in a conditional discharge for twelve months and here he was appearing yet again, some eighteen months later.

The Chairman of the Magistrates decided that the transgressor wasn't going to be 'let off' this time and had determined to impose a substantial financial penalty. The way that he passed sentence however provided a great deal of amusement for everyone in court. His sermon of reproach went something like this:

"You've done this before on three other occasions, when you were bound over and conditionally discharged but here you are, before the court again for doing the same thing. We have decided that this time we are going to deal with you more seriously and we are determined to make you feel it through your pocket."

Many of the solicitors on the front bench could not contain themselves and had to leave the courtroom. Mr Croft, on the other hand, had totally missed the point.

When the eleven-thirty list had been dealt with there was no one else left and even then at ten past twelve, with the greatest of ill-will my case was called on.

"If this case isn't finished for one o'clock you will have to come back at half past two," said Mr Croft.

"Bollocks!" I said to myself, "You ignorant bastard!" But then modesty forbade me to say it.

"Of course, but I would rather hope that we manage to deal with the case before then," I said politely.

I made a bail application for Danny, purely and simply because both of my clients insisted on it, but it was with the greatest reluctance. It was true that Danny had denied the offence, it wasn't his house and there was no independent evidence to show that he had actually sold any of the drugs, and to be fair the case against him was very weak.

The Bench retired and Mr Croft was not called for.

They returned just before one o'clock, which meant that I would be able to get to Rotherham for the afternoon court.

Davina was remanded in custody, having made no application and remarkably Danny was bailed, subject to fairly restrictive conditions.

I went to see Davina in the cells afterwards and expressed my concerns.

"It's all right Mr Smith, I'm going to use this prison sentence to straighten myself out and come off the drugs. Danny is going to get us a house in another area and when I'm released we'll settle down. Danny says we will get married whilst I'm in prison."

I smiled and nodded but made no reply.

I returned to Rotherham and wondered what Davina's parents would have thought had they been there to see their eldest daughter become a jailbird.

On the way back in the car I was struck by a very personal melancholy. I wondered if it really was a good job after all; had I wasted all the years of training, reading and learning; did I actually serve a useful purpose; did I help the administration of justice? My answer to each question was in the negative and for the first time I began to have serious doubts about the adventure I had undertaken in the Law. For the past few months I had dealt with nothing but Junkies, Judges and Jail and I was sick and tired of all three.

45

In view of Davina's pleas of guilty and the fact that she had accepted full responsibility Danny's pleas of not guilty were accepted and he was released from the court scot-free. Davina's case was adjourned for four weeks so that she could see a probation officer and a report be prepared to tell of her background and her present circumstances. I was convinced she had 'taken the rap' for Danny, but she would have none of it.

She said that if he had been convicted he would have got six years because of his record, whereas she would get less as she had no record and so they would be apart for a shorter period if she admitted the offences.

She was right, the Judge sentenced her to three years imprisonment, saying that it was a deterrent sentence to show other drug-dealers that the court meant business. He had got it wrong but I was powerless to intervene as my suspicions were irrelevant and after all, in the court's view she was just another junkie asking to be put away.

I asked her if Danny appreciated what she had done but she maintained his innocence, saying that their relationship would rise above the sentence and the opinions of an 'out of touch' judge. I suppose I was out of touch too, the times were definitely changing and, I regretted, for the worse.

My last comment to Davina was to the effect,

"I hope he's worth it."

"Yes, he certainly is," she said defiantly.

I just nodded. She must have thought I agreed.

I lost contact with both Danny and Davina after the case with the exception of a letter which Davina sent to me from prison a fortnight after her sentence, in which she requested that I help her recover some of her clothes from the cells in Goole.   She told me that she'd come to terms with the sentence, that Danny was visiting her regularly and whilst he did not wish to get married in prison, he was making arrangements for this to take place upon her release.   She made no mention of her sister or her parents, but did say that she was finding the deprivation of liberty difficult to deal with.   I wasn't really surprised.

Approximately nine months later I was walking near to Clive's jewellers in Rotherham when I saw Danny Newton walk out of the front door, and I thought for a minute he was with Davina because from the back it looked exactly like her.   But then I realised she couldn't possibly have completed her sentence, unless she had got parole so I decided to catch them up to see how they were.

They stopped outside the café next door where they were joined by another young lady who was busy looking at a ring on Danny's escort's ring finger.   As I drew level I heard the words,

"Congratulations to you both."

Fortuitously a group of people came out of the café which prevented their seeing me and as I walked to the side I was surprised to see that the girl was not Davina, but someone who looked very like her and I had not seen before.   I also noticed that she was heavily pregnant.   I stopped to look for a second or two before guessing that my presence would probably not be welcomed and so slipped out of view into the next road.

Danny now has three children by this lady, although they are separated and he lives with someone else.   I have not seen Davina since that day at the Hull Crown Court and neither, I understand, have her parents or sister.   She served eighteen months of her three-year sentence.

Chapter Three

Anyone for Cricket and Watch Out for Wardle

June is supposed to be a month of good weather and the term 'flaming June' comes to mind. So it was in 1984.

I was due at the Abbeydale Cricket Ground, Sheffield, to watch Yorkshire play a county match as the guest of the great Jarvis who had ordered the tickets for me and my partner Steve Wilford who, I might add, was more interested in the boozing than the cricket. Our builder friend Bodger Broome, who was taking the day off from a small contract he had at Jarvis' house was joining us together with TenBelly Norman, the gourmet and beer-drinker supreme; Louis Frame, the mad Scotsman; Timbo Johnson from the Bradford and Bingley Building Society and Mike Walker the then manager of Whitegates estate agents in town and bringing up the rear none other than the Havana cigar smoking entrepreneur and insurance broker Sean Page. These were all members of our 'inner circle' who had devoted themselves to hard work and the pursuance of a good time.

The arrangement was that a mini-bus would take us to the ground and bring us back in the early part of the evening. Inevitably I had to make my own way because I had the morning court, but then I always had the morning court whether I liked it or not. It was a peculiar position to be in because on the one hand I wanted to be out with my pals, but on the other insecurity forced me to keep a presence in the Rotherham Magistrates Court arena.

I was hoping to finish my list by about 12 noon and be at the ground for lunch whilst my colleagues on the other hand were meeting at 9am and would be at the ground by 10am.

Everything was going well until Trevor Wardle walked into my life. He was to an easy working day what Hitler was to origami.

He had been up to his old tricks of fiddling one-armed bandits and breaking into cars, although he claimed that he had turned over a new leaf and had decided to try to join the army. To prove his point he produced a copy of an application form which had a list of questions referring to the applicant's health and hereditary illnesses which was to be submitted to a locally based regiment.

Under the section relating to health, a number of conditions were listed with the forewords "Have you or any of your immediate family suffered from any of the following, and if so, state the relationship of the sufferer."

Amongst the list of complaints was the term 'congenital heart disease'. Good old Trevor had ticked that and at the side of it he had put the word 'stepfather'!

I thought I had better point out the inaccuracy in his reply so I set about trying to explain.

"You see Trev, the fact that your stepfather has congenital heart disease is irrelevant. You see, they want details of *your* family history."

Trevor thought for a minute and just when I thought I had got through to him he spoke.

"What's irrelevant mean?" he asked blankly.

"That doesn't matter," I continued, "Your stepfather is not a blood relative is he?"

Trevor thought again.

"E's a relative though by marriage i'nt 'ee?"

I realised this was going to be difficult.

"Well," I said, trying again. "If your father was bald and your grandfather was bald it's a safe bet that you will follow the family history and go bald yourself, do you see?"

Trevor thought again.

"Me father wasn't bald, he still isn't, so I'm alreight there aren't I?"

"No, that's not what I mean, you see........."

"My stepfather is bald though," interjected Trevor.

Feelings of annoyance were setting in when in frustration I just asked,

"Do you know anything at all about genetics?"

"Yes," said Trevor triumphantly. Tamla Motown, great group, love their music."

I decided not to press the point further.

"There was one of them with big......."

"Yes, I know who you mean," I interjected, "But listen, for the purposes of this form, family means the same blood."

"Same blood?" said Trevor in a state of confusion.

"Yes. You see, your dad if your dad and your mum is your mum."

"Correct!" shouted Trevor, believing he was being clever

"So," I continued, "Anybody related to them in the blood-line is a relative so far as this form is concerned, OK?"

"OK," said Trevor confidently.

"So your father in law is not a relative for these purposes, OK?"

"Why not?" asked Trevor.

I dismissed thoughts of bending a steel RSJ over his head and imagined what his interview with the army might be like. I shuddered and saw no point in persevering.

"There is one thing," said Trevor.

"What's that?" I asked.

"The genetics were before Tamla Mowtown, weren't they?"

I decided that guilty pleas were appropriate to all Trevor's charges and so when we went into court he said 'Guilty' to each of the four matters and the Magistrates decided that they wanted a Probation Report preparing before they dealt with him. Adjourning a case in this way is a procedure where the Probation Service prepare a report about the background of the Defendant and then see if they can come up with some form of recommendation as to what the sentence should be.

As I was being given the date for the adjourned hearing, Trevor tapped me on the shoulder. I stopped what I was doing and turned around to see what pearls of wisdom were going to come forth from his fountain of knowledge.

"Don't forget to tell them about the army," said Trevor.

"Would that be British or Salvation?" I asked.

"British, definitely British," said Trevor as he sat back in his seat with a self-satisfied look on his face.

We left the court and Trevor wandered off down the street, oblivious to the fate that was to befall him four weeks later when he was given a three month sentence, thus missing his appointment with the army.

I left the courtroom only to be called back in by the emphysemic usher who told me that a prisoner had been brought into the cells, arrested on warrant and he had asked for me.   A warrant had been issued for his arrest because he had failed to attend court on the due date, so I went down the spiral staircase to the cell area whilst I waited for the jailer to make his appearance.   I could hear him on the telephone referring to some 'twat' or other and hoped that the reference wasn't to me.

He appeared at the gates and queried who I wanted to see.

"I'm not sure, but it's a new prisoner who's been arrested on warrant."

"Ay, another bleeder – more paperwork to fill in.   Why can't they turn up on time, the bastards?"

He opened the door and continued chuntering and issuing forth various swear words.   I on the other hand attempted to make light of the situation and speak as though I was happy and contented.

"Not to worry, we'll soon be out of here and home Derek,"

"Like bleeding hell you will.   Got another of the bastards that they've picked up coming in in half an hour.   Been on the run, the bastard, he ought to be shot with shit.   I'd drown these buggers and shove a red-hot poker straight up their jackseys.

"Splendid, splendid," I said, congratulating him upon his humanitarian standpoint.

The jailer opened the cell to the executive suite otherwise known as cell three with the iron bed and broken toilet and out came a dishevelled, rather sick looking youth called David Selby.   I noted that he had what looked like burn marks down the side of his face and his hand was similarly marked.   The side of his head was also burnt and the hair had not grown back properly, so it did not take a Sherlock Holmes to work out that he had been involved in some sort of fire.

I took him to an interview room and as I did so the jailer continued to chunter under his breath, disputing the parentage of every one of the prisoners that afternoon.

Selby sat down opposite me with what seemed a permanent sneer on his face and it was soon apparent that he had 'an attitude problem'. He threw some charge sheets onto the table and I looked at them to find that he had been charged with the attempted theft of copper cable, to which I added further details from him when the true horror of what had happened was explained to me.

Apparently he had been on some banking of earth on the way to Sheffield and had seen workings which had uncovered some large thick copper cable, the dream of every would-be tatter. A tatter is a man who collects scrap metal, copper being particularly popular because it has certain value to the scrap trade. The charge was quite old and it had taken some time for the matter to get to court which confused me, so I probed a little more deeply into the background.

Selby told me that he was not guilty of the offence, although I should add at this stage that the majority of Defendants are not guilty, or certainly that's what they tell their solicitor and the trick is in getting them to admit their guilt when it is clear there is no prospect of an acquittal. You are actually doing the Defendant a great favour because he can only make matters worse by pleading not guilty when on subsequently being found guilty after a trial, the court will give him little sympathy for not admitting it in the first place.

There are of course cases when a solicitor will advise his client to plead not guilty if the evidence is not strong but such cases are few and far between, bearing in mind the screening policy now operated by the police and the Crown Prosecution Service, as they will not prosecute a case unless a conviction is likely.

Selby's story was fantastic. He expected me to believe that he was walking his dog on the banking when it ran after a rabbit. In his haste to retrieve the dog, he slipped down the bank on some mud and as he was gathering momentum he reached out to grasp something to break his fall. Unknown to him the 'something' was a metal saw which then came into contact with the copper cable and there was an explosion.

"An explosion," I said incredulously.

"Yes," said Selby, "You see the cable was live and was carrying power from one pylon to another. I was blown up into the air and suffered serious burns to my face arm and body. When I came to I was in the hospital where I was told that I had been electrocuted. They said it was a miracle that I hadn't been killed. My hair has been curly ever since."

I could not resist a smile.

"You mean to tell me that you grabbed a saw by accident and again by another accident the saw ran across some copper cable, cutting into it, and in the process you were electrocuted?"

"Yes," said Selby enthusiastically.

I always tried to temper my enthusiasm for my job with a measure of self-control and courtesy to the client, so I choose my words carefully and respectfully.

"That's the biggest load of bollocks I have ever heard," I announced.

"You don't believe me, do you?" said Selby disappointedly.

"Correct," I said, deciding not to mince words. "You see I really don't think the court will believe you either."

"Why not?" he countered.

"Because, not to put too fine a point on it, your story is……..well, it's crap."

Selby looked hurt and I realised I had probably offended him, so I tried to re-establish some credibility.

"I'm only trying to help you David," I said sympathetically.

"Well, believe me then," he said sarcastically.

I have always found that a high percentage of criminal clients will not face up to the inevitable and will wriggle and argue black for white until the cows come home, but at the end of the day the court will impose a greater sentence if they feel they have been messed about.

"David," I continued, "If you plead not guilty you will lose the case and probably your liberty as well."

"Do you mean bird?" he asked.

"Yes, bird," I replied, using the slang word for prison.

"Fuck me!" he said exasperated.

I shuddered at the proposition.

"Just understand, I won't mislead you."

"No, but tha doesn't give me much confidence."

"What would you have me say to give you the confidence I want?"

"Say I'm going to get off."

"OK, you'll get off."

"But you don't mean it."

"That is correct."

"But that's not right is it?"

"That's also correct."

"Oh, fuck it!"

"You only hear what you want to hear and when you don't get what you want you take your bat and ball home."

Selby hung his head and began to sulk. The bat and ball had gone and the stumps were on their way too.

"I'm running it. I'm not guilty and I'll get off with it."

"Well not with me you won't"

"That suits me. I'll get a solicitor who will fight, not someone who gives in."

"Well, I wish you the best of luck."

"I don't need it, I'm not guilty. There's no way they will find me guilty of this. Anyway, thanks for nothing."

"OK David, I hope you get what you deserve."

"I will, don't worry about that."

"Oh, I'm not worried, I'm just sure."

Selby had missed the point entirely so I gave him his papers and he left the office in search of another solicitor who would do his bidding. He was going to have a long search but then there's always someone who is short of work and will be prepared to bite their lip to get the case; by contrast I had got to a stage in my career when I wasn't prepared to be told how to do my job by a nerd like Selby. It wasn't arrogance but just a little self-respect.

I left the cells and dropped my files off in the office before setting off for Abbeydale and the cricket.

It was twenty past two by the time I got there but when I reached the hospitality tent the lunch had been cleared away and the only drink left was a medium white wine, which I hate, so I settled for a glass of iced mineral water and went off in search of my friends.

I took a casual walk around the ground but with the exception of bumping into some business colleagues I could not find Pagey and Co anywhere.

I recognised one chap in blazer and cream trousers who worked in Rotherham and had fallen asleep in the sun with his head on one side, so I woke him to discover that the left-hand side of his face was bright red whilst the right hand side was white and pristine. He had visited the brandy bottle on a few occasions and whilst he did his best I couldn't quite understand what he was saying.

I asked him if he said seen Pagey, Jarvis or Goody, during which his head wobbled in a 360° motion and then with a great effort he began to speak again. I recognised the name 'Page' and the word 'bar' so did not need any other information before setting off in search of the members' stand. Sure enough, my instincts were right as there in a corner of the bar were the gang, Pagey, Jarvis, Goody, the mad Scotsman Lewis Frame, Bodger and Bader, who had been joined by insurance men Andy Lovell, Dave Eastwood and Ray Pink. Wilf was sitting on a stool at the bar sharing a pack of cigarettes with another insurance man Dave Hill, who was affectionately known as 'Over the'. They were listening to the latest joke from Tim Johnson of the Bradford and Bingley whilst another reprobate Julian Binney went around the group collecting for the kitty.

Bodger told us that he had a cert at Haydock Park called Method Actor, or something similar and he had been told by a former jockey that it couldn't fail.

"Why is he a former jockey?" I asked.

"He was suspended for illegal betting."

"Oh, marvellous! I suppose he's the most reliable source."

"Not 'alf," said Bodger confidently.

"Anyway, what are the odds?" I asked conveniently forgetting our source's suspension.

"Eight to one," said Bodger, "But that's now. I don't know what it will be in an hour's time."

"Let's have a go," shouted Pagey, "£5 each."

Everyone else agreed but Wilf beckoned me towards him.

"Lend 's a fiver."

"Bloody hell Wilf, you took £25 out of the petty cash this morning."

"Yes, but I had to get the first round."

Begrudgingly I handed over a £5 note together with my own and Pagey volunteered to go to the bookies, after all he was the expert.

I was very hungry so I bought a pork pie from the bar and watered it down with a pint of Guinness. I must admit it was wonderful.

It was 3pm and not one of us had seen a ball bowled, so at 3.30 we decided to go into the ground and enjoy an hour's cricket before tea. It was idyllic; the sun was shining, the air was dry and warm and the gentle breeze carried the smell of freshly mown grass. I was sitting with my pals with a pint of Guinness in one hand and the remnants of a pork pie in the other, amidst surrounding fields which were a stunning mixture of greens from bright emerald to a soft bronze.

"At its best this country takes some beating," I announced proudly.

"It certainly does," said an Indian gentleman wearing a turban, sitting next to me, which prompted us to enjoy a long conversation about the beauty of our respective countries until a large cloud moved quite quickly across the sun, blocking it from view. Further clouds moved in the direction of the ground so that within twenty minutes it was quite dark and just as I was about to warn the group of the prospect of rain, it started. Within seconds the stand was emptied, apart from the chap with half his face suntanned, who had given me directions earlier. He was fast asleep and had begun to get very wet although surprisingly the droplets of rain had not disturbed him. I imagined that within minutes he would be soaked, but no one wanted to risk the rain to tell him. Within minutes his white Panama hat was flattened around his face, rather like a teapot cover. Pagey thought it was hilarious.

We watched the television in the bar as Method Actor romped home by three lengths and we all had £50 each to come, or we would have if Pagey had backed it! He thought that Pile Driver was a better bet and thinking he was acting in our best interests he had put all our money on him.

Following his confession, the members' bar was treated to a chase around the ground as Pagey tried to escape the clutches of a number of highly emotional, if slightly inebriated punters, one of whom tripped over the spectator with the Panama who was still asleep on the boundary, seemingly enjoying his sleep in the rain.

Chapter Four

Spider's Reunion

Michael Wellington McIvor, otherwise known as Spider was one of my most loyal clients, having a face, ravaged by the meandering of the local tattoo artist's needle which haunted me throughout the early days of my practice. His forehead bore the words 'Ford Cortina Mark IV' after the favourite motor vehicle of the local villians. The large tattoo, which dominated his face, was of a spider which was hidden in an even larger web extending from his cheek to his neck and about his chin were small spiders, completing the family portrait gallery.

Despite his aggressive looks Spider was an inoffensive and careworn youth, disowned by a little-caring mother who had no idea who his father was, let alone her so-called responsibilities to her child and she had slipped into drunken oblivion when Spider's usefulness had ceased after the Child Benefit had run out.

For the most part he had lived in a variety of childrens' homes until he reached the age of eighteen years when he was in turn replaced by another fatherless clone of the ever expanding sub-culture of subversive children with no hope and even less future. Remarkably, however, Spider was not bitter and he often spoke in glowing terms of his mother as 'simply gone away' to recuperate after a long illness.

Unfortunately his desire to be noticed caused him to pursue this objective by debauching his face with the said series of tattoos and this had served to haunt both our existences.

He became a local joke, his true character being submerged in his search for notoriety, but he wasn't really a thief and certainly was not violent.   I doubt if he had a malicious bone in his body despite the revulsion that many people felt at the sight of him, and the endless taunting he suffered from his peers.

Spider had a lonely existence enhanced only by unscrupulous rogues who used his longing for friendship to their best advantage and such was the direct route into drugs.

I often wondered why kids, or indeed anyone for that matter, took drugs.   Was it just curiosity or was it because our modern culture decreed it was macho to take them or perhaps it was peer pressure and the desire to share their self-induced addiction so that they were not alone in the slippery slide to misery?   Whatever the reason, the so-called 'designer' drugs featured in cases in the criminal courts with an alarming degree of regularity, so much so that it made one's head spin to see the same faces with the same problems and only the names changing, as the conveyer belt of drug related crime dominated the lists.

Another name entered the criminal dictionary; the 'junkie' had been born and was living in Rotherham as well as just about everywhere else in the United Kingdom bringing with him addiction, drug related crime, the Legal Aid lawyer and Her Majesty's Judges who, when all else failed, sent them all to prison.

The sequence was simple and quickly established as an order of priority from junkies to judges to jail and I was seeing a lot of all three.

People like Spider were easy meat for the drug barons who plied their evil trade with wanton disregard for all who fell within their wake and Spider had already spent two periods in prison. This served only to consolidate his own addiction imposed by those who chose to use him as a small-time pusher and delivery boy on behalf of those who preferred to keep their fingers and criminal records clean by letting some other fool take the risks and the blame when the police came to call.

I was sitting in my office late one afternoon, having enjoyed lunch with the great Jarvis and David Bader Lidster, when Tracey told me that Spider had come to call.

"Mr McIver," I announced attempting a hospitable welcome.

"Hello Mr Smith," replied Spider in a tone of resignation which left me in no doubt that he was in trouble and my intuition proved right as he produced a handful of crumpled carbonated pink pieces of paper to prove it. He was in possession of five South Yorkshire Police charge sheets alleging that he had possessed and intended to supply Cannabis, Heroin and a remarkably long named drug called Methylenedioxymethylamphetamine, better known as Ecstasy.

The intriguing thing was that there was no allegation of actually supplying the drug to anyone specifically and the evidence of intention to supply was inferred from the quantities of drugs which had been found in Spider's possession. In other words, there was far too much for one person to use and accordingly the likelihood was that he must be selling it to others.

I completed a Legal Aid application and then proceeded to question him as to what plea he was going to enter.

"Guilty," said Spider firmly.

"I think we've had this conversation before," I replied.

"What do you mean?" asked Spider suspiciously.

"Just what I said," I continued, "You don't expect me to believe that you had approximately five thousand pounds worth of dope entirely for your own benefit do you?"

Spider made no reply.

"Some time ago you were sent to prison for two years for drugs matters. Do you remember that? I represented you and I was quite satisfied that you were covering up for someone else at the time. I think you are doing exactly the same now."

"Whose side are you on?" shouted Spider.

"Your bloody side," I shouted back, trying to contain my temper. "Can't you see I am trying to help you. You'll go down for at least four years this time and what will your druggy friends do for you then? ..... Bugger all!"

"I did it and it was mine," said Spider.

"I don't believe you," I said.

"It's not what you believe," said Spider sarcastically.

"If you expect me to believe that then you can go and be represented by somebody else. If you think I am going to let you take the rap this time, then you are nothing more than a bloody idiot!"

As soon as I'd said it I regretted it, and never more so than when I saw the hurt in his eyes. Everyone else had called him an idiot, ever since he was a child, and there was I, his solicitor and confidante and someone who should know better, treating him exactly the same as everybody else.

Spider looked down at the desk with his head bowed, avoiding eye contact and slowly he reached out with his right arm to take hold of the charge sheets, then rose from his seat, still with his head bowed, and walked out of my office.

"Shit!" It was the only thing I could think of to say.

A fortnight later I was in the Magistrates Court when the emphysemic Usher coughed and cleared his throat and then coughed again as he called out the roll-call of names of Defendants who were to grace Court One with their presence. I recognised one name in particular.

"Michael Wellington McIver," shouted the Usher rather demonstratively and Spider answered.

There was a ripple of laughter along the court corridor as Spider came into view behaving almost like a leper as he looked to the floor in an attempt to conceal his face. I was surprised to see he was represented by one of my competitors and when he came into court he listened intently as the Prosecutor read out the facts of the case, referring to a large quantity of drugs which had been valued at over five thousand pounds. How on earth would Spider have been able to acquire five thousand pounds worth of designer drugs unless he was a courier? The proposition defeated all reason and I had no doubt that he did not have the gumption to sell them himself, so once again some smart alec supplier had escaped justice on Spider's back.

As I listened to the outline of the allegation it became apparent that the Magistrates would decline to deal with the case, and sure enough after the hearing the facts they announced that the Crown Court was the appropriate venue on the basis that their powers were insufficient to deal with it.

The case was adjourned for eight weeks during which time the CPS would prepare the case papers before serving them in time for his final appearance at the Magistrates Court and his committal to the Sheffield Crown Court itself.

Here I suspected he would appear before some grumpy Crown Court Judge who disliked junkies and Spider would be despatched into the arms of the Governor of Leeds Prison at a rate of knots.

As Spider left the court he looked at me momentarily but his face gave nothing away and within a second he was gone.

Later that day I was at the police station and by pure coincidence I ran into Detective Inspector Lightowler of the Drugs Squad who was new to the area and wanted to be a Superintendent. In the belief that convictions led to promotion he had flung himself heart and soul into his work and Spider was child's-play for a policeman for he admitted the offences without any prefabrication.

"It's over for McIver," said Inspector Lightowler knowingly. "He hasn't briefed you has he, so why should you be interested in his fate? You know we've got him game, set and match." I saw no point in arguing with him.

I realised that the police had simply accepted his admissions and had closed their file but they had got it wrong for Spider was nothing more than a messenger boy. His difficulty was that in taking the blame for someone else he had lost a deal of his mitigation and the court could only sentence him on the basis that he was indeed guilty of being a mainstream supplier.

On the following Wednesday evening it was the weekly soirée with my beloved football team who were to play the Probation Service: a group of caring gentlemen who worked hard to reintegrate criminals into society. They had great patience and a wide tolerance level to be able to cope with the stress of dealing with sometimes hostile people who were less than honourable. But when it came to the football field, they changed and I sustained more injuries playing against the Probation Service than any other team as they relieved the frustrations and stresses of their day. Solicitors were very similar in attitude however and so the net result was that the football ground became a battlefield.

Bader Lidster was our captain for the night and owing to absenteeism we had drafted in his two brothers, Barry and Peter, to strengthen our defence. Barry was a very skilful player who always seemed to have plenty of time to make the ball do just what he wanted and his brother Peter was extremely quick on the wing, with a turn of speed which would leave you gasping. Peter, or Lefty as he was known (because of his proclivity for using his left fist to hit defenders), was on majestic form and by half-time we were 3 – 0 up.

During the tactical team talk we all drank copious quantities of Lucozade whereas our goalkeeper, Big Norm, drank two cans of Guinness, and although he was not a particularly good goalkeeper, he weighed in at eighteen stones, which seemed to give him the ability to be able to 'narrow the angles', using his huge frame to get in the way of the ball. He was one of those players who either had a good game or a very bad one, but in this particular match his positional play was inspired, even if he did annoy everyone by sipping from a can of Guinness during the match itself whilst urging us on with cries of, "Lame him!" or "Kick his head in!" when a member of the opposing side committed a foul.

His constant references to the opposing centre-forward as being a 'shirtlifter' brought a rebuke from the referee and when he caught sight of Big Norm drinking Guinness, he ordered the can be taken from the pitch. Fortunately the referee did not hear Big Norm's eloquent repartee when he reacted by shouting,

"You bald-headed twat, I'll shove this can of Guinness up your arse!"

Quite how the referee would have managed that manoeuvre was beyond me.

The game ended at 4 – 2 in our favour, although it should have been 4 – 1 but for the fact that their last goal was scored whilst Norman was at the side of the goalpost urinating with his back to the play when a back pass from Bader Lidster trickled into the back of the net. Understandably Bader was most put out and he ran up and remonstrated with him,

"I'm somewhat disappointed with that rather bad show of goalkeeping Norman," or words to that effect.

We adjourned to the bar after a shower and the niggles and annoyances from the match disappeared over a couple of pints of beer, with Norman very much the brunt of sarcasm from the rest of the team for his faux pas. The Probation Service enjoyed our hospitality, particularly the pork and dripping sandwiches from the canteen, which we had named 'Cholesterolville', so that everyone except Norman and Bader went home happy.

The following morning I woke up suffering with pain in my big toes caused by my ingrowing toenails and the constant booting of the leather football and Probation Officers' backsides. I limped up to the court, a rather forlorn and partially lame individual but en route ran into Big Brenda Dobkin and her Rottweiler/Alsation cross known affectionately as 'Tiger'.

The dog looked placid enough, although I didn't stroke him just in case and was humoured by seeing his tail wag furiously during the conversation.

"'E's a good boy," said Brenda in a deep resonant voice, which would have inspired many a male voice choir.

"Yes, he looks OK," I replied cautiously.

"Aye, 'e is but he hates postmen. Every time he sees one in his posty uniform he goes mad and tries to get at him."

The dog then licked my hand rather affectionately, leaving it full of slaver.

"Look 'ow 'e is, 'e loves you."

"Yes, I can see that," I said as he shook his giant head, coating my trousers with copious amounts of slaver.

"But you watch 'im with a postman's uniform, 'e goes berserk."

"Why is that?" I asked.

"Don't know. I reckon one must have kicked him when he was young. They don't forget you know."

"No, of course."

The animal shook its head again but at least now my trousers matched.

"Anyway, I'll see you again, OK Brenda?"

I went off up the court steps.

On my arrival I saw a corridor full of the usual suspects, a veritable rogues' gallery representing the seamier side of the Rotherham criminal classes. There were Defendants who were there purely for motoring offences who stood out like sore thumbs, resplendent in their best suits, sporting attaché cases, clutching their Summons, their hand-written sheets of mitigation and letters of support from their Area Managers. The other half of the clientele were resplendent in jeans T-shirts and trainers which had seen better days, clutching other people's attaché cases which they had nicked earlier on. I shouted out the names of my clients greeting the ones who answered and then discussing the issues of the day, i.e. how we would be proceeding with their cases.

Unfortunately the three courts sitting that morning were all occupied with other cases, so it gave me some free time to visit the WRVS canteen which was situated in an anteroom off the main corridor. They sold a variety of biscuits and sweets together with an array of hot drinks, such as tea, coffee, chocolate, Bovril and an imposing mixture made out of Oxo cubes and hot water, served in polystyrene cups.

Terry Jordan Fitzgerald was sitting in the tea-room heavily engaged in reading one of the glossy pornographic magazines which had the word 'nudist' in the title. Terry's name had the ring of an author about it but he could not claim to be so distinguished as the only thing he had ever written was a forged sick-note for one of his court appearances. Terry was over six feet tall and weighed about nineteen stones. He had a shock of carrot-coloured hair, a dreadfully spotty complexion which had never seen a hint of Clearasil in his twenty-four years on this earth and with his buck teeth he looked like a giant rabbit. He was a small-time crook, specialising in thefts from motor vehicles and what he did not know about tyres and wheel-trims was not worth knowing.

Despite all his failings he was quite a likeable rogue, best described as an unintentional comedian, because he had the ability to make people laugh without realising it. His biggest problem was a stutter which seemed to affect certain letters of the alphabet more than others, often

69

leading you to think he was about to swear, particularly on the letter 'F'. I decided to engage him in conversation.

"Well that's very nice of you Mr Fitzgerald, I'll have a tea with two sugars if you please," I said cheekily.

"You can f... f... f... f... fetch your own tea, tha's got more money than me."

I was struck by Mr Fitzgerald's sparkling repartee and so decided to treat him.

"I suppose you'll want a cup of tea then Mr Fitzgerald?"

I don't think he heard me, as his attention was fixed firmly onto the middle page of his magazine. I acquired two pristine polystyrene cups full of a dark brown liquid posing as tea and sat beside him.

"I have not got any whisky with me, so it's straight tea Terry," I said.

"F... f... f... f... fine by me," said Terry who then returned to his studies.

I looked over his shoulder at his magazine and saw a variety of pictures of men and women of all ages, shapes and sizes in a variety of unusual poses, attempting to look as though they were not posing and were acting quite normally, hanging out washing in the garden in the nude.

"I didn't know you were into naturalism," I said seriously.

"F... f... f... f... found it on this bench."

"Oh," I replied with a grin, "I thought you were going to put your name down to join one of their clubs."

"F... f... f... f... forget it. I couldn't walk about like that," he said pointing to a youthful but rather nubile young woman with flaxen hair who appeared to be purchasing an ice-cream from an equally nude vendor.

"Well, I wouldn't imagine you'd look like that anyway Terry," I said sarcastically, "And besides you don't have a bust."

Terry grinned and continued to read.

"What you in for then Terry?"

"F... f... f... f... found a tax disc and coppers say I nicked it."

"Theft by finding then Terry is it?"

"F... f... f... f... forget it, it's not nicked and I'm going to tell 'em. Will it take long?"

"Probably," I said, "Especially if you represent yourself, but then do your best."

Terry looked up briefly from his studies and in passing said,

"F... f... f... f...".

I was out of the door and on my way to court two before I heard what he had to say. When I had finished my case in court two I wandered off to the rathole at the end of the court corridor and fought my way through the smoke and the grime, stepping warily over outstretched feet. There was one face in particular which stood out. It was Michael Wellington McIver and he appeared to want to speak to me.

"Can I have a word Mr Smith?" asked Spider.

"Yes, of course Spider, come on in," and I took him to the interview room.

"I've just come to say sorry that I 'ad seen another solicitor," said Spider.

"That's all right Spider, no offence taken I can assure you," I said, lying through my back teeth.

"Well," said Spider, "I want to change back to you again. I don't like this bloke, 'e treats me like a knob-head."

I couldn't help thinking that that was because Spider was a knob-head, but I was overtaken by sympathy.

"Well you can change if you want Spider, but that is entirely a matter for you."

"Well I'd like to change back to you because you know me and my background and I've always got on well with you."

I was pleased by Spider's loyalty, something normally quite alien to many of the characters of the people we had to represent.

"I have got some good news for you," said Spider.

"Go on then," I said, ever the sceptic.

"I've signed myself in for a detox," said Spider, "It starts tomorrow."

I was delighted and I told him so.

"I am sick and tired of drugs," continued Spider. "I don't think it will take long because I've not been out long enough to get back into it in a big way. My Probation Officer 'as fixed it up for me to go in to the 'ospital and I am going to give it a go."

"Well done Spider," I replied.

"There's one other thing as well," said Spider, "Do you think that if I get these tattoos off my face they will stop laughing at me."

I asked Spider if he was serious and it appeared that he was. I couldn't help but admire him for his intentions.

"Yes, Spider," I replied confidently, "I think they will."

We finished our conversation and Spider set off for the clinic.

A fortnight later and purely out of interest I rang his Probation Officer to see how he was getting on, to be told that he had completed his detoxification programme and his last urine sample had revealed the absence of opiates confirming that there were no drugs in his system. He had subjected himself to weekly tests and had honoured the appointment with the plastic surgeon concerning his tattoos.

Over the next four weeks whilst Spider was waiting for his case to come up at the Magistrates Court he had tested negative for drugs at each check and a date for the first operation on his face had been fixed. Spider was brighter and happier than at any time in his life, but the icing on the cake was that the Probation Service had found his mother living in the south of England and attempts had been made to reunite them.

I could not help thinking how tragic it was that within only a matter of a few weeks Spider would be finding himself serving a sentence in one of the local jails, but if it wasn't too long there was the prospect of him being reintegrated into a society minus his tattoos and drug addiction.

On the day he reappeared at the Magistrates Court for his committal to the Crown Court, Spider was as happy and content as I had ever seen him before. He had been drug free for almost two months and he was about to go into hospital for the first operation for the removal of the tattoos. He had been given a date for the Crown Court some eight weeks hence which would allow time for him to have the operation, meet again with his mother and take up the offer of a new job as a gardener which the Probation Service had managed to find for him.

I was conscious of having built up a considerable mitigation, but whilst I didn't feel it would save him from an immediate prison sentence, I recognised it may well shorten it. One Monday morning Spider telephoned me to say that he was moving his address and he wanted me to know where to contact him. He also told me that the drug barons with whom he had previously been associated had ascertained his whereabouts and had paid him a visit to say they were none too happy at his 'retirement' but he had resisted their advances at the cost of a black eye and a broken nose. He had declined to make a complaint to the police but had had the foresight to see his Probation Officer who was doing his best to have him rehoused. I complimented him upon his resolve to free himself from the drug scene but I know the harsh realities of life were often difficult to accept as the Barons would do everything they could to bring Spider back into their employ.

Some weeks later on the eve of Spider's appearance at the Crown Court I received a copy of his probation report which would be used at the Crown Court hearing. It was an extremely favourable document, telling of the enormous strides which he had made by resisting his drug dependency, and confirming that for the fourth consecutive month he had tested drug free. He had started work at one of the old folks' homes working in the garden and had recently been rehoused into permanent accommodation. Arrangements had been made for Spider to see his mother and he had asked me if he could use my office as a meeting place because his flat was part of a house shared by a number of others, which did not lend itself to the necessary privacy or hospitality. He did not wish to meet her at Social Services premises for that was the venue of their meeting before their separation and consequently he had no one else to whom he could turn for support. I therefore set aside one of our large rooms for the meeting and placed a coffee machine inside for their use whilst Tracey collected some sandwiches and a couple of cakes from a local shop, which were then left on the desk.

I returned from court at 1pm to find Spider sitting in my reception area dressed in a new suit, white shirt and a pleasant tie, which had clearly been selected for him by someone with dress sense. His hair was short with a side parting and his face and hands were spotlessly clean. He had used some form of cream on his hair to stop it looking like a hayrick but whilst it looked smart it accentuated the dreadful tattoo on his forehead and face, despite his attempt to conceal them by layer on layer of foundation. He was sitting nervously on the edge of his seat as if waiting to be interviewed by the C.I.D. but as I opened the door to enter the room his face lit up and he couldn't help but ask me what I thought of his appearance.

"You look very smart Spider I have to say, in fact if that suit was a bit bigger I'd borrow it off you."

Spider laughed.

"What time is she due then Spider," I asked.

"Anytime now Mr Smith," he replied. "I haven't seen her for years you know so I don't suppose she'll recognise me in this suit."

"No, I don't suppose she will Spider I replied. "Does she know you've got those tattoos?"

"No," said Spider, "That's the main problem. I don't think she'll be very impressed, but I've got a letter here to show that they are being taken off."

"Very good," I said, "But if you'll forgive me I've got to do some dictation, so feel free to wait here for her and stay in the room for as long as you want."

As I turned to leave, Spider called after me,

"Thanks very much Mr Smith," he said, "I'll not forget you for this."

"That's all right Spider, I am happy to oblige. Anyway, you deserve it for the efforts you've made. By the way, how's the job going?"

"Oh, it's great," said Spider, "Although the old people were a bit put about when they first saw me, so I wear a woolly cap right down above my eyes so they can't see the tattoo on my forehead."

Looking at the tattoos everywhere else on his face I wondered what they thought about them, but the lad meant well and after all they would soon be removed.

I went into my room and saw Wilf reading the paper and drinking a glass of Canadian Club.

"I'll have one of those," I said, and Wilf promptly poured me a treble. We discussed Spider's visit including my foray into social work but then Wilf reminded me that, that very evening, we were due out for one of our monthly soirées with Bodger Broom, the great Jarvis, the mad Scotsman Lewis Frame and the inimitable Sean Page. The petty cash was systematically plundered in the knowledge that the meal would not be expensive, but the drinks bill probably would be.

Having prepared for the afternoon court session I left the room just as an elderly lady with dyed blond hair, black at the roots and a careworn face which was heavily lined, walked into reception. She wore a faded coat, her shoes were down at the heel, and she had all the frailty of appearance of an old-age pensioner, but then Spider disturbed my observations with a shout.

"Mother!"

The lady simply replied, "Michael" and there was one of those pregnant pauses when the film on the screen moves into slow motion as Spider and his mother embraced and then they started to cry. I urged them into the room which had been set aside for their purpose without introducing myself to the lady then closed the door, winked at Tracey and set off for court.

Spider's meeting took about three hours, but when I got back both he and his mother had gone, although apparently their re-union had been a great success resulting in the pair of them going out for the rest of the afternoon when they made all sorts of plans for Spider to visit his mother's home in the south of England. The whole day had been a sizeable hit with the only blot on the landscape being the spectre of the court proceedings, or at least that's what I thought. But I was in for a considerable shock.

Chapter Five

Fitzgerald Faces F... F... F... Jail and Spider's Fond Farewell

"Terrence Jordan Fitzgerald to see you," said Tracey sharply. She was wearing a purple number with a tight-fitting top and pencil skirt, complimented by purple tights and purple shoes with a brass buckle. As ever she looked extremely smart, with accent on colour co-ordination and as she left the room Fitzgerald turned his head to survey her from the rear when the expression on his face indicated a measure of satisfaction until he sat down in front of my desk and his concentration returned.

"To what do I owe this honour Mr Fitzgerald?" I asked.

"It's the police, they have f... f... f... fetched me another summons for another tax disc and when I was in court last time the f... f... f... foreign-looking magistrate told me if I came back he'd send me to f... f... f... jail.

"Then why did you do it Terry? You were only in court two days ago."

"I'm f... f... f... 'fraid it just 'appened. I saw another tax disc and I picked it up."

I looked at his charge sheet and realising the totality of his dilemma I addressed him again,

"Yes, you picked it up all right, you picked it up whilst it was still in a motor car and you've been charged with pinching that as well."

"It's not f... f... f... fair," continued Fitzgerald, "I only borrowed it because I 'ad 'urt my foot and I couldn't get 'ome. I didn't think my mate would mind me borrowing it."

"But you don't have any insurance for this vehicle either do you?"

"I've f... f... f... found my mate's insurance policy, but it doesn't cover me."

"Brilliant!" I said, "So you've got theft of a tax disc, taking a motor vehicle without consent, no insurance and oh, what's this?" I said noticing another piece of paper hiding in the envelope, "Oh yes, giving a false name to the police."

"F... f... f... false name?   I gave him my mate's name, that's not false."

"No, it's false to you, you twerp.   What did you get when you were last at court?"

"F... f... f... fifty pounds fine."

I couldn't resist it.

"That's not f... f... f... fair."

Terry smiled.

"It's not as bad as I'm going to f... f... f... get this f... f... f... time."

"Too f... f... f... true I thought to myself!"

I completed the documentation before sending him on his way.

"By the way," said Terry as he was leaving.

"Yes?" I replied.

"Is she courting?"

"Who?" I asked.

"Your receptionist."

"Why?"

"I f... f... f... fancy her."

"Oh," I replied, "I think she'll be pleased," I said sarcastically.

"Does tha' think so?" asked Terry.

"No, I don't, you're too old for her." I was joking.

Terry thought for a minute before replying

"Would she fancy a f... f... f... fair old night out? I'll take her to the dogs."

"I'm sorry Terry," I continued, "But Tracey has got a boyfriend."

"Can he f... f... f... fight?"

"I shouldn't think so, and why should he?"

"I just wondered, if it came down to a scrap."

"I don't think it should come down to a scrap. What's the matter with you, that proves nothing except who can fight and who can't?"

Terry looked at me as though he had fallen dumb because he could not understand my comments at all; such was life in his jungle. The strange macho desire to fight had been with us since Neanderthal man and here he was alive and well and stuttering in Rotherham.

As he was leaving, Tracey walked in and Terry winked at her.

"'Ello baby, do you like big boys?"

"No, do you?" replied Tracey sharply.

"F... f... f... fancy that! She's quick i'nt she?"

"Only if you're following me," said Tracey even more sharply.

Tracey's repartee floored Terry and he gave it up as a bad job, but not before blowing her a kiss which she ducked to avoid, leaving him to shrug his shoulders and inform me that she was 'playing hard to get'. He left the office whistling the old song *'Mr Wonderful'*.

When he was out of sight I engaged Tracey in conversation.

80

"He likes you Tracey," I announced.

"Thrilling," she replied dismissively.

"But he does. I think he wants to take you to the dogs."

"And that's where I would be going if I went out with him," she replied.

"I just thought I would mention it," I said.

She left the room whistling the theme tune from the film *'The Great Escape'* and I got the distinct impression she was not interested.

Wilf joined us with the early edition newspaper and pointed out that we had lost £5 because Monte's Revenge had come fourth at Haydock Park. As he was reading the sports column I was drawn to the front page which was staring me in the face from across the desk. One of the headlines read, 'Local youth dies of drug overdose'. I looked intently at the paper until Wilf finished reading the sport and put the paper down on the desk, when I picked it up and read on.

'Twenty-one year old found dead in flat. Police say the death is being treated as suspicious.'

The next paragraph took my breath away

'Michael Wellington McIver was found unconscious last night by his landlady. Police were contacted and he was taken to hospital but found dead on arrival. The police have asked for anyone with information to contact any police station.'

Just at that moment I was disturbed by a telephone call from D.I. Lightowler.

"Hello Mr Smith, I'm ringing about Michael Wellington McIver. I wonder if you can help me?"

"What can I do?" I asked, in a state of shock.

"I take it you know…..?"

81

"Yes, I've just read the paper.   What in goodness name happened?"

"Well…..I'll call round if I may?"

"Yes, certainly.   I'm going out in half an hour, so is there any chance…..?"

D.I. Lightowler interrupted me.

"I'll come round now."

Desmond Lightowler was a success story and was regarded in police circles as a 'high-flyer', having risen to the rank of Detective Inspector within a very short time, but rapid success such as his attracted enemies from both the private sector and the police force itself.

Lightowler was one of the new breed of policemen who had taken a Law Degree at University whilst on the police force payroll, passing with flying colours.   His ambition was to achieve the highest rank possible and everyone in police circles who knew him thought he would do it, unless his enemies got to him first.

He was an imposing figure of over six feet tall, plain of face but bright of eye, with tightly cropped black hair and he had the sort of swarthy look, which would require two shaves each day to remain clean and tidy.   He was a snappy dresser, always wore a suit and a shirt with a highly starched collar, tied his ties with a Windsor knot which was never out of place and his shoes were always highly polished.   It was said that his marriage had been ruined by his relentless pursuit of a career and I was soon to find that he was one of the most determined men I was ever to meet. If he had weak links in his character it was his cynicism and arrogance which did not endear him to many and he spoke with an air of aggression, which could be quite intimidatory; a feature which he used to his best advantage.

What you saw was what you got; he was hard and uncompromising and unfortunately rather heartless.

My preparation of the character study was interrupted by his speech.

"Thank you for seeing me Mr Smith," he said politely but didn't mean. "I am involved in the McIver death investigation and I'm making some enquiries. I wondered if you might be able to help me?"

"If I can," I said, "In what way can I assist?"

"Well," continued Lightowler as he looked around the room making a mental note of its contents, "I have been unable to contact McIver's mother. She lives in Northampton but she's not at that address and I'm led to believe that she's staying with some friends in this area with a view to meeting her son."

"So she doesn't know then?" I asked.

"Not unless she's found out from some other source or has read the paper, but I wondered if you had a contact address."

"I've got a note of it somewhere, although I didn't have a reason to keep it. Strangely enough I think it's in one of my notebooks. I'll look if you like."

"Yes, I'd be grateful if you would," said Lightowler, and I set about searching through a mass of papers. As I was looking for the number Lightowler spoke again as he inspected my certificates on the wall.

"Funny job this one," he said quizzically.

"Yes?" I said. "The papers said you were treating it as suspicious. What's happened?"

"Well, I shouldn't really be divulging information, but being as you were his solicitor, he's got hold of some

Heroin and taken too much of it.......yes, looks like an overdose."

He stared at me intently, almost as if looking for a reaction and then he spoke again having noticed my facial reactions give myself away.

"You don't think it was anything else do you Mr Smith?" he asked cautiously.

"I'm afraid I can't help you with anything other than my own suspicions."

"What are they?" asked Lightowler, with his head leaning to one side as if straining to hear an answer.

"Well, I understand that Spider was off drugs.   He'd been tested negative in his samples for a good few weeks now."

"And how do you know that?" asked the Inspector.

"His Probation Officer told me, and in addition he was working.   If he'd been back on the drugs I'm convinced they would have known about it."

"But these druggies can't pack it in," he continued.   "They often promise great things and some of them can keep off it for a day or so but sooner or later they are bang at it again.   They can't keep off it you see, no character."   D.I. Lightowler's stiff upper lip was showing.

"I take it you don't accept that Mr Smith?" he asked noticing my reaction.

"No, I don't.   It just doesn't stack up.   He'd been free of drugs for a number of weeks, he'd got a job, he was seeing his Probation Officer regularly, he had just been reunited with his mother.   Everything was going for him so I just cannot see any reason for him to return to drugs, unless….."   I paused momentarily to allow my mind to consider the proposition.

Lightowler's interest was aroused and he turned away from my certificates on the wall to face me with his eyes sparkling in anticipation.

"Unless what Mr Smith?" he asked.

"Well I know that he was frightened of the Drug dealers who'd been using him and he had to move address to get out of their way."

Lightowler shook his head dismissively.

"Well, they probably found him and flogged him some more dope, he took it because he'd been off it for a while and he took more than was wise for him."

I didn't have the information to enable me to argue with the Inspector, but I had a gut feeling about the case and I couldn't believe that Spider had taken drugs voluntarily.

"Well I don't exactly have a great deal to work on," continued the Inspector.   "No one appears to have seen him that day and there are no witnesses who can help me as to any visitors that he may or may not have had, so in short we're left with the simple conclusion that it was an overdose, for whatever reason."

"I don't doubt that it was an overdose, but what I'm concerned about is how he came to take it," I countered, not realising that I was rising to his bait.

"Are you suggesting that somebody killed him?" said the Inspector in mock indignation.

"It's just that I don't believe that he was back on drugs and I don't believe he would have taken it of his own volition."

"Well as you know Mr Smith, we cannot prosecute on gut feelings."

"Of course Inspector," I said, "I'm more than well aware of that, but you asked me my opinion and I gave it.   If you don't like it you shouldn't ask."

The Inspector nodded and smiled in the knowledge that he had touched a nerve.

"Have you got the number then?" he asked, changing the subject.

"Look, maybe it might be better if it were to come from me. I of course infer no disrespect but I have at least met her on one occasion and she knows of me."

The Inspector thought for a minute before replying.

"Yes, if you like, it's a job less for me and not a pleasant one at that, but er........would you ask her to ring me on this number?" he asked passing me a card.

The Inspector turned to leave, but then pretending is was an afterthought he addressed me again.

"Oh, by the way, you don't know the name of these drug dealers do you?"

"No, I was never told I'm afraid."

"No, I suppose he kept it to himself," said the Inspector. "I'll check through his files and see what I can come up with. If I find anything I'll let you know."

"Thank you for that," I said.

"Yes, well I'll be off then. No doubt our paths will cross again," he said knowingly.

"Yes, no doubt they will."

The Inspector paused as if trying to find something to say, so I broke the silence in the hope that he would go.

"Well, cheerio then Inspector."

"Yes, cheerio," he replied and with that he was gone.

He was the sort of man you couldn't help but dislike.

Just then Wilf returned to the room.

"Who was that?" he asked.

"Why do you ask?" I replied.

"Well he saw me holding the glass of whisky and he looked as if he wanted to analyse it and me as well."

"Well it's a good job you're not driving as he's probably waiting outside. He's a policeman."

"Ah, I thought he was," said Wilf, "He had that look about him .....big feet. By the way, that's sad about poor old Spider. Tracey's just told me, she's quite upset."

"Yes, it certainly is," I said slowly gathering my thoughts.

"He'd just seen his mum again hadn't he?" asked Wilf.

I didn't reply but just nodded.

"Does she know?"

"No," I replied.

"Who's telling her then?" asked Wilf.

I didn't reply but just looked at him.

"Oh no, not you.......rather you than me old chap," and Wilf then left the office.

I took the piece of paper from the notebook and dialled the telephone number which was answered almost immediately. The voice on the other end of the phone was not Mrs McIver but a friend of hers and she promised to pass on my message that she should call to see me that afternoon. I didn't say why but I placed enough importance upon what I said to ensure that she call back, and indeed a little before five thirty that afternoon Tracey came in to tell me that Mrs McIver had arrived.

I had a small glass of whisky before I went to collect her and having invited her into my room noticed she looked brighter than when I saw her before. There were no black roots showing, she had had her hair done, was wearing a smart new coat and what I concluded were a new pair of shoes, because I could see the still clean price label on the sole of the right foot from where I was sitting. Before I could speak she began to tell me of her exciting reunion and her plans for her own and her son's future. I could not get a chance to speak.

There's something very strange about bad news, and I'm not sure whether it's body language or facial expressions but she seemed to realise that something was wrong, because suddenly she paused and in doing so stared into my eyes as if the answer were there.

"It's Michael isn't it?" she asked gravely after a second or two.

I didn't reply immediately since there was no easy way to tell her that her son was dead. The bond between mother and son is unique, no matter how the relationship has floundered in the past and it was almost as if she had some sixth sense or premonition of what I was about to say.

I took another deep breath, but before I could begin my sentence she had already realised what my reluctance was concealing.

"He's dead isn't he?"

I looked at her blankly before nodding and waited for a response, during which Tracey brought in a cup of tea, having anticipated the grim duty which I had to perform whilst Mrs McIver maintained a blank expression, almost as if she'd been paralysed by some lethal injection.

I reached for the small whisky bottle out of my cupboard and poured her a glassful. After a second or two Mrs McIver seemed to come out of her trance, looked at me but politely declined the drink, saying that she had agreed with Michael she would give up alcohol in return for his giving up drugs. She asked for an explanation and I did my best to placate her, with my view.

She asked that no further questions or comments be made and then slowly, but not reluctantly, she got up and left the room without speaking.   I spoke to her at the top of the stairs as she was leaving and offered my assistance in any way that I could, when she forced a smile but simply closed the door behind her.

I watched from my window as she walked down the street and into the arms of a woman who I assumed was her friend.   During the space of a second or two they embraced each other for what seemed like an age.

The tree-lined drive into the crematorium had been a solemn pathway for so many cortèges over the years and would continue so during my lifetime until inevitably we all take our turn in final tribute.   I saw an official wearing black with pinstripe trousers walking to his office with a sprightly gait.

"What a job," I thought to myself.   "I wonder if he thinks about his final party?"

He looked at his watch and at the roadway leading to the gates as he waited for his next guests, rather like an hotel manager, with a reassuring plastic smile and a courteous nod hiding the temptation to shout, 'next please'.

I sat on the back row on the left, watching intently as some seven or eight mourners listened to the words of the Reverend Blanchard, who with consummate courtesy spoke of the efforts Spider had made in coming to terms with his addiction and all his other problems.   The good Reverend did his very best to find something really pleasant to say to a small gathering of faceless people whom I had never seen before.

Mrs McIver clearly consumed by grief was sitting at the front being consoled by her friend, her cheeks flushed, her eyes reddened with crying, and I suspect feeling more than a fair share of guilt. I noticed the familiar face of the Probation Officer, also Spider's Social Worker, and in addition there appeared to be a young man of about Spider's age. Sitting on the opposite row and in the corner at the back was the familiar figure of Detective Inspector Lightowler.

The service was short and yet poignant and when it ended the gathering left with the eerie sound of the sixties pop song *'Kites'* by Simon Duprey and the Big Sound playing in the background .

There was one funeral car and as I was standing in the doorway I watched Mrs McIver and her friend drive away from the crematorium steps, up a long winding path to the large gates until out of sight. Within seconds a further funeral cortège for some other unfortunate entered the crematorium and the whole sequence started again.

"This is everybody's destiny," said Lightowler grimly, disturbing my thoughts.

"Yes, it's not much to look forward to is it............it's even worse when it ends like this. Anyway, what brings you here Mr Lightowler?" I asked.

"Just thought I'd pay my respects so to speak and see who might have turned up."

I had absolutely no doubt Lightowler had come to the service to see who had turned up, but I wasn't too sure about the former proposition, and yet it intrigued me that he had attended at all. I wondered if he'd taken on board some of my comments and whether or not there might have been some suggestion of foul play.

"If you hear anything on the grapevine so to speak," said Lightowler, "Doubtless you'll keep me informed."

"Of course," I said, "You already know my views."

"Yes," said Lightowler, "I do."

Lightowler forced a half smile before striding off in the direction of the car park and after a moment or two I walked up the long winding path myself in the same direction. I was struck by the peace and tranquillity of the area and the order and tidiness of the flower beds which would hardly ever be noticed in this place which I prefer to avoid.

As I drove off I saw a red sports car parked on its own at the far side of the car park, with an open view of the gates and the chapel itself, but I could not make out the occupants, who seemed to be reluctant to show themselves – or perhaps it was just my imagination. I continued my walk and shuddered without explanation as I drove through the main gates to arrive back in Rotherham in time for the afternoon court where I was to represent a drug supplier whose case was first in the list.

Chapter Six

Return of the Prodigal and What a Gay Old Party This Is!

"Why should I plead guilty when I haven't done it!" shouted Fifi DuPont, the Sheffield prostitute and thief who was denying being a Sheffield prostitute and thief. "What would I want with a Black and Decker drill?" she protested.

"The mind boggles," I thought, but I didn't say it as I listened intently to a tirade of complaint, whingeing and controlled aggression from the ageing Miss DuPont, who took her surname from a sailor who knew her mother.

"The last thing I want you to do is to plead guilty to something you haven't done, but I do ask you to consider the evidence of the store detective."

"Bollocks!" came the reply.

"No, the store detective. He says he saw you pick up the deodorant stick and push it down your cleavage."

"He didn't see that at all," she persisted angrily. "If that was the case I would have had three tits! Come off it...... grow up.......get real........he never saw that........he couldn't ever see me from where he was, he would have had to have seen round corners, and he can't do that, not while he has a hole in his arse."

I realised that Miss DuPont had a nice turn of phrase and as she continued to vent her spleen I couldn't help wondering what the purpose of reading and studying all those law books was, only to be told that there was a possibility that

Derek Morgan, the store detective, may well find his anal canal sealing itself with the passage of time.

"He ought to go and fuck himself," she continued.

"Would that he could," I replied wearily.

"You what?"

"Nothing. I'm just wondering why he would say he saw it if it wasn't true. What has he got against you?"

"He doesn't like me."

"You don't know him."

"I saw him watching me....dirty bastard!"

I realised there was little point in arguing with Fifi whilst she was in that mood, because as a pathological liar she had talked herself into believing her innocence and to have pushed the point further would have only caused her to lose confidence in me and promote bad feeling between us. It was time to back off and try again another day. It is always difficult for a client to admit his or her guilt, particularly if they had just spent time trying to persuade you that the contrary was true.

Fifi was an unusual woman, with a character moulded by circumstances and the path upon which life had led her. FiFi, or Janet Wadkin as she was know on her birth certificate and at the DSS was placed in a home at the age of eleven, had her first child at thirteen and then started 'on the game' at fourteen, which she had played ever since. She was thirty-six years old, going on sixty, and with her best years behind her she was staring oblivion firmly in the face and there was nothing she could do about it.

Of her the old maxim was true – 'a person who cannot trust is a person who himself cannot be trusted'.

She had come too far and witnessed the very worst that the excesses of the human condition had to offer, but hard as she was, I could not help but feel sorry for her. She was one of life's great casualties but didn't really know it.

She was five foot nine inches tall, with dyed blonde hair whose roots were just beginning to show through and her make-up comprising the mandatory bright red lipstick of her profession combined with dark eye-shadow to render her almost clown-like in appearance.

She had dull lack-lustre eyes heavily shrouded by eyelids which had begun to sag, perhaps implying the onset of a squint, but she had pleasing high cheekbones and an endearing dimpled chin which was quite attractive. She had kept her figure and a ridiculously short mini-skirt revealed a pair of shapely legs draped with fishnet tights. Overall the picture was of a common prostitute, which was unfortunate because despite everything Fifi had an exceptionally high I.Q. which regrettably she had not chosen to use in a more moral perspective.

Somehow I had to re-establish myself in her eyes because she was beginning to think I was 'just like the rest', evermore willing and able to criticise or find fault, so I changed tack.

"I've been told you have a high I.Q." I pronounced profoundly.

I noticed I had struck a chord, Fifi's ego was alerted causing her defences to go down as she shrugged her shoulders and failed to answer.

"Why didn't you stay on at school?"

"I was brought up in a home and I had to leave," she replied quietly.

"What did you do when you left?"

"I got a flat and went to work."

"Where at?" I asked, not expecting the answer I was to get.

94

"On the streets you burke, where else? What is this, twenty questions?"

"But why?"

"Because it was the easiest thing to do," she replied, "And the money's good."

Her eyes narrowed as she spoke and at that moment she was more rational than at any time in the conversation.

"I was wrong of course, but it's too late now," she said contemplatively.

"It's never too late."

"Oh yes it is, I couldn't change if I wanted to."

"What about your father?"

"Who?"

"Your father."

"He was a nice man but mother was cruel to him. She kicked him out when I was seven and that's when the uncles started to come."

"Uncles?"

"Yes, uncles, you know who I mean. Well, she had to survive somehow didn't she?"

"Did you ever see your father again?"

"No, he came for me once but I was in the Home then and they wouldn't let me out. He said he would come back for me, but he never did."

"And you haven't seen him since then?"

"He came to see me again when I was about twenty, but I moved around you see and changed my name to duck the police and the DSS. I didn't actually make it easy for him did I, but then I was on the game proper and I didn't want him to see me like that, so I pretended not to be in."

"You're joking," I said, "You hid from him?"

"Yes.   It broke my heart but what would he have thought?"

"Don't you think you owed him more than that?"

"Yes, don't you think I haven't paid for it.   That poor man. But I can't put back the clock," she said dejectedly. "That's why I never talk about it, it upsets me."

For the first time I thought I saw the hint of a tear and the possibility that she was human after all.

"But he must be sixty now?"

"Sixty-four," she replied, "He's sixty-five at Christmas. On the 24th of December to be exact."

"Where is he now?"

"I don't know.   He moved away, someone said down south, but I'm not sure."

What's his name?"

"Martin Wadkin – Martin David Patrick Wadkin to be exact."

"Have you every wondered about him?"

"Every day – every single day."

I had touched her suppressed conscience and she tried to change the subject but I wouldn't be deterred.

"Why don't you find him?"

"What would I say?   Hello Dad, I'm a prostitute and I have convictions to prove it.   Oh and by the way, I'm a thief as well and I have a drink problem and I'm a liar too…this is just how your daughter has turned out.   Now don't ask me any more."

"I'm sorry but the story is so sad, it seems such a waste, just think of it….."

She interrupted my line of thought.

"You know, if you had a drink I would think more of you than I do now."

I poured her half the contents of a can of lemonade.

"Have you got any whisky?"

"OK," I replied, "One tot with my compliments."

"Thanks Steve," she said, taking the glass carefully so as not to spill any of its contents. She drank it in one gulp, placing it on the end of my desk with considerable panache.

"I'm off now. We've finished haven't we?"

"Yes I suppose so, but I want you to think about your plea."

"You want me to go guilty don't you?"

"I want you to put the best case you can without sticking your neck out because if you fight and it goes wrong you will get a heavier sentence which in your case could mean prison. Then you'd blame me."

She smiled, realising what I was getting at, as more often than not criminals blame their lawyers if they are sent to prison. But Fifi was bright enough to see I was advising her for the best.

"Can you get Cannabis in prison Steve?" she asked.

"Of course, there's not much you can't get in prison. The only thing you are denied is your freedom."

She smiled again and nodded knowingly. Once again she had taken the point.

"And besides there are some funny women in prison – you wouldn't like it."

"I'm going now. All this talk of prison and funny women is depressing. I'll see you as they say, in court. 'Bye for now."

She blew me a kiss, winked, pushed back her hair and left the room.

I couldn't help thinking how it took all sorts to make a world, but then Tracey came in and passed me some more letters, amongst which one in particular stood out because I recognised the writing. It was post-marked Newcastle and we had had to pay an excess charge to the Post Office, since whoever sent it forgot to put a stamp on.

Who could this be from, as if I didn't know? Yes, it was a missive from Mr Albert Heptonstall formerly of this parish so I opened the envelope with care because knowing Albert anything could have been placed inside.

I unfolded the rather grand-looking letterhead which clearly belonged to an expensive hotel and then read the contents.

> *Steve,*
>
> *It's me, Albert.   Ow are u.   I'm all reight. Mother's all reight and others are all reight and snake dog and goat are all reight – we are all all reight.   Are u all reight?   I ope u are all reight cos if u are we are all all reight.*
>
> *By the way me pigins are all reight but dads not all reight.   He wants to kome back, cant settle so we are floggin the pigins and am komin bak ome. Dad as spoke to counsil and we are taking an exchange so I'm waiting for a moovment.*
>
> *Thall niver guess were komin back to t same streat that's great int it.   Anyway we are komin ome next munth so we avin a party and want thee to kome.*
>
> *Dad said thall be pleased so I think tho should no fust.*
>
> *See thee next munth.*
>
> *Albert*

PS   Grandads all reight but is piles are ruff, poor old bugger

I couldn't help but smile, and in fact I was downright pleased - apart from Granddad's piles of course.   To say that I had feelings of unrequited joy would perhaps be an overstatement, but apart from the fact that half my criminal practice was returning to me, I realised I would actually be pleased to see Jack and Albert with the rest of the Heptonstall clan back in Rotherham.   I believe in fate and the remarkable thing about the Heptonstall's return was that they were able by a most incredible stroke of luck to return to the same two council houses which they had occupied prior to their departure, as these occupants wanted a move too.   Apparently when they returned Billy One-Leg, their aptly-named next-door neighbour, was said to have looked out of the front window and uttered those immortal words of welcome,

"Oh bleeding 'ell, they're back!"

Fortunately Jack did have his admirers and a number of partisan colleagues (some of whom were fully employed in the criminal professional and some of whom were not) would welcome them back with open arms.

A street party was organised and I was invited to what could only be described as a remarkable occasion.   The entire street was bedecked with small triangular flags on never-ending cords of string, which were draped from bedroom to bedroom across the street itself.   The flags were of a white background and on my arrival I scrutinised them carefully to find the word 'Woolworth' written in red ink in the middle of each one.   Tables were set out in the street holding an array of foodstuffs, from sandwiches to pork pie, sausage rolls and similar delicacies.   One of the brightly coloured tables was standing outside Jack's house and contained similar objets d'art of the food world but also included one plate full of the most awful-looking items I had ever seen.

On my arrival Madge greeted me as though I was a long lost friend. She was a middle-aged woman whose best days were behind her, with a careworn face, heavily lined but substantially camouflaged by a mask of jet black hair streaked with grey. She had massive wrists and a powerful grip which made me wince as she shook my hand violently.

"It's good to see you again Steve," said Madge enthusiastically.

"Me too Madge and welcome home. Rotherham just hasn't been the same place without you."

"Smashing," she said, her brain working overtime thinking of something pleasant to say.

"'ave a whelk," she said handing over the plate with the odious looking contents.

"Our Albert's favourite, them. 'e loves whelks, particularly fried-up with a bit of mash."

Noting my attempt to cover my revulsion she spoke again.

"Just try one then Steve and see what yer think. If it's crap, spit it over Billy One-Leg's wall."

She smiled as she spoke, which caused her to open her mouth, so displaying a ridge of gum which stood out all the more for want of teeth. There could be no doubt she was Albert's mother.

"These'll put 'air on yer chest," said Madge.

"Do you eat them Madge?"

"All the time," she said, "They're great, but they make me a bit windy."

I dismissed visions of a hairy-chested Madge with a bad bout of wind from my thought processes and to avoid causing offence I took one of the ghoulish-looking objects, and plunged it into my mouth. I pretended to chew it vigorously, making noises of culinary satisfaction but when she wasn't looking I surreptitiously removed it and flicked it over the fence into Billy One-Leg's garden, then I moved off rather quickly on hearing someone shout some unpleasantries.

Jack made his appearance wearing a bright red and white Caribbean shirt which failed to match the green and white football shorts, but this bizarre outfit was ultimately to be outdone by the addition of a pair of hiking boots draped over the tops with white sports socks. He entered to wolf whistles from the growing crowd who had gathered to fight their way to the front of the food queue.

Jack passed me a paper plate and urged me to fill it with whelks, but I declined politely and made for the chicken legs, which had been beautifully stacked in the shape of a pyramid. I took two such items and a dripping breadcake as an old lady who introduced herself as Albert's grandmother, passed me a small bowl of a steaming decoction better known as Madge's famous stew which I found quite pleasant upon the taste-buds. I ate it all apart from a strange looking object in the bottom which looked remarkably like a whelk.

As I was eating my last sandwich Jack engaged me in conversation whilst acknowledging so many of the gathered throng.

"What do you think to your whelk stew Steve?" asked Jack, seeking praise.

"Very nice Jack, it's a most unusual dish, but very tasty."

"Ay, it is," said Jack.

"I thought I could taste stew-meat?" I questioned.

"Argh, tha can," replied Jack.

"Why is that?"

"'cos it's got stew-meat in it," said Jack with a straight face. "Just wait a minute," he continued as he turned to Madge. "Madge?" he asked earnestly, "Have you seen my pile ointment?"

Madge had not quite heard what he had said.

"Have I seen your what, Jack?" she asked.

Jack shouted at the top of his voice, "My pile ointment."

This comment caused a number of the guests to turn and look in bewilderment and caused me to replace two grapes I had just acquired to the dish from whence they came.

"It's in a pot next to the Fiery Jack in the bathroom," said Madge.

"Right," said Jack, "I'm going upstairs to put some on, I can't sit down, reight!"

A number of diners seemed most put out by this verbal outburst but as Jack moved off Madge seemed to be reminded of something so she shouted after him.

"Be careful because they're in the same colour pots."

Jack didn't answer but I presumed that he must have heard what Madge had said.

I was engaged in conversation when Albert appeared, eating what seemed to be the remnants of meat from a bone which was formerly a leg of lamb.

"Eh up Steve," said Albert, "Thanks for coming. Do you want a whelk?"

"Hello Albert," I said, declining another plate of shellfish, "I'll pass on the whelks and I'll have one of those custards," pointing to what appeared to be a delicious array of confectionery. Albert reached out for a custard and took off the silver foil as he handed it to me.

"You ill-mannered little bugger," said Albert's grandmother, "You should always offer food by handing over the plate.

"Oh, righto Grandma," said Albert, who then picked up a paper plate, took the half-eaten custard out of my hand and placed it on the edge, handing it back to me with a grin.

"Ee, that lad," said Grandma Heptonstall. "What can you do with him?"

I pondered on the question for a moment as I was taken over by thoughts of tying Albert to a tree and flogging him with a cat o' nine tails, or electrocuting him with an extremely high voltage.

I was then treated to a flagon of home brew, a sickly-looking substance which Jack and Albert had been fermenting over a period of time from an idea they had picked up when watching the film, *'The Great Escape'* where the American prisoners of war had found a way of making 'hooch' by some manner of distilling the juice from potatoes. It occurred to me that they would need a licence to carry out such a process, but I did not have the energy to try to explain it and I must confess that the brew had a certain joie de vivre.

I then tried a glass of home-made punch, with a cherry and a piece of carrot in it. This was another of Jack's remarkable concoctions and my first mouthful removed most of the enamel from my teeth. The other half of the glass found itself over Billy One-Leg's fence. I was then introduced to the Local Council Housing Manager's representative; a nice bloke of middle years who was tall, thin, had a black moustache and wire-rimmed glasses. I realised that Jack was right when he told me that he was a 'dead-ringer' for Doctor Crippen. Jack had plagued his life incessantly during the time that he was trying to retain his council house and to show his appreciation he had invited the man, whom he knew as Zed, to the party. Zed explained to me that he had turned up purely and simply out of relief that Jack had ceased to telephone him every day.

He wore a tweed sports coat and cavalry-twill trousers, and favoured thick-soled shoes. Carrying the customary brown brief case that had seen better days, if you had had to pick his profession, you would most certainly have said that he had come from the Town Hall, and of course you would have been right. I had a brief conversation with him, but after he had dealt in finite detail with the problems surrounding the Housing Office in Rotherham it appeared we had exhausted all avenues for suitable topics of conversation so I moved on. I asked Albert why they called the Housing Officer 'Zed', only to be told that it was because he was always asleep when anyone wanted to see him.

Just then Jack came back to see us but appeared to be in extreme discomfort.

"I am walking like bleedin' John Wayne," said Jack, his face grimacing in pain.

"Yer don't ever want these piles," said Jack, "They make your life a misery."

I agreed with him thinking if I did have piles, I would want some of my own and not his, but then Jack spoke again,

"Madge, where is that bloody pile ointment?"

"I've told you, it's in the bathroom cupboard. There are two containers, one's got pile ointment in it and the other…….."

Jack interrupted her.

"I need somebody to put the ointment on."

I looked away from his gaze in the sincere hope that he wasn't considering that I would play doctor, but Madge intervened before Jack could ask me.

"It's time for a song Jack."

Alreight then," said Jack, "Where's our Ven? He can start and I'll join in when I've put some ointment on."

Ven was one of the younger siblings who had a pronounced stutter, but remarkably had an unusually pleasant singing voice. His stuttering seemed to disappear completely whilst singing which prompted me to suggest to Jack that in future he should sing his conversations and they wouldn't take so long; an idea to which Jack agreed but whose funny side he failed to see.

Ven announced his song, which took a considerable period of time owing to this terrible affliction, but when he broke into the strains of *'Unchained Melody'*, made famous by a pop group from the 1960's called The Righteous Brothers I was amazed at the quality of his voice, even if his hip gyrations were a little over the top. When he had finished his song he received tremendous applause, together with shouts of 'more' from Dr Crippen from the Council who, by this time, was on his third glass of punch.

Ven graciously introduced another song, which took even longer than the last introduction and there followed an excellent rendition of *'Why Must I be a Teenager in Love?'* which had been recorded by the great sixties star Craig Douglas, whose acquaintance I was to make some years later. Everyone joined in the refrain, including Dr Crippen who by this time was on his fifth glass of punch holding a glass in one hand and a small plate of whelks in the other.

Another rousing reaction from the audience prompted a third and final song which was the Martha and the Vandellas classic, *'Dancing in the Street',* urged on by an extremely tipsy and exuberant Dr Crippen from the Council, now on his seventh glass of punch.

The whole street entered into the spirit of the occasion.

".......it doesn't matter what you wear just as long as you are here, so come on now around the world............"

I couldn't remember the rest of the song and neither could any of the others and so the song ended with

".......la-la-la, la-la-la-la..........dancing in the street."

Towards the end of the song Dr Crippen gave us an unexpurgated version of the twist, which caused him to fall to the floor and gyp unmercifully as his stomach rejected the onslaught of Jack's punch and fried whelks. As the audience were patting him on the back Dr Crippen leaned over Billy One-Leg's wall and vomited fiercely. All I could hear were cries of 'never again' from Crippen and finally, 'Bleeding 'ell, what do you think you're doing you dirty twat?' from Billy, at which point it was clear that Billy One-Leg was not impressed either with Dr Crippen's arrival or his contribution.

"He's not a bad lad, that kid from the council," said Jack, "But he can't hold his liquor or his whelks."

I looked on passively and nodded in agreement as Madge attended to the stricken council operative by offering him a cup of black coffee with another whelk, which induced poor Dr Crippen to vomit once again over the same wall, and prompted Billy One-Leg to lose his temper.

"You filthy, ugly, twisted little twat!"

"Shut thee face," said Jack, "Just because tha's not bin invited there's no need to throw thee weight abart, so put a sock in it, tha should 'ave one spare!"

Billy One-Leg was not impressed with Jack's repartee but it was obvious that Jack couldn't care less and he sat down beside me to tell me of his health problem, describing his condition as the 'grapes of wrath', which I thought was a famous book by John Steinbeck, but to Jack it meant something entirely different.

"It's no good," said Jack, "I'm going to 'ave to put some of that cream on.   I'll need a handful for these little beauties," and with that he was gone.

Just then a young girl appeared, who I assessed to be around 16 or 17 years old.   She had an extremely pretty face, bright blue eyes and a beautiful complexion.   She quickly became the centre of attention as she walked almost surreptitiously to where Albert was standing, put her hands over his eyes and shouted,

"Guess who?"

She looked longingly at Albert and for reasons which I failed to grasp she was clearly smitten with him.   Being beautifully dressed and well-spoken I couldn't for the life of me understand her fascination for Albert, who by comparison had been thrown out of the ugly competition for being too ugly.

"Oh, 'ello Caroline," said Albert despondently, "What are you doin' 'ere?"

"I've come for your party.   Your mum invited me last week."

"Oh, good," said Albert without meaning it.   "Do you want a whelk?"

"No thank you," said the blonde beauty, "But I thought it might be nice if we could go for a walk, the park is beautiful at this time of year."

Albert looked at me and then looked at the heavens, almost for inspiration.

"I can't go now," said Albert, "It's me dad's party. Come back another day."

Caroline was clearly upset by the rebuff but Madge had heard the conversation and interfered.

"'ello Caroline. Thank you for coming. Our Albert will go up to the park with you a little later, won't you Albert?"

Albert looked at his mother with some disdain, but her wrists were thicker than his and so he simply nodded his head with marked reluctance.

"Oh, good," said Caroline. "I must say I enjoyed Ven's singing.

"Oh, ah," said Albert.

"Yes, he's got an excellent voice, and how remarkable it is that the stutter disappears once he starts to sing."

"Ah," said Albert looking up to the heavens as if seeking an escape route.

"I bet you're a good singer too Albert," she continued.

"Ah," said Albert.

"Not as good as he is at conversation," I thought to myself as I looked on helplessly.

Shortly afterwards Caroline went into the house to help with the washing-up, striding over Dr Crippen in the process who by this time had taken to resting on the pavement in a horizontal fashion.

"Is that the new girlfriend then Albert?" I asked.

"No, it's not," snapped Albert. "She's just an 'anger on."

"Anger on?" I questioned.

"Ah," said Albert, "She's a bloody nuisance.   She's always trying to get me to take her out.   She asked me to go to the library the other day.   I asked her what the bleedin' 'ell do I want to go to the library for, it's full of books.   She said there was a nice café in there, but they didn't do sausage rolls or chips so it couldn't be that good."

"It seems to me Albert that she's genuinely fond of you." I said.

"Bollocks," said Albert, "She's a nuisance."

"I've noticed a lot of the other young men here looking at her with admiring glances."

"Well let them take 'er to the library then," he replied.

"Do you mean to tell me you don't like her?"

"Yes, I don't like 'er".

"But she's gorgeous."

"Ah, but that's not all."

"What do you mean Albert?"

"It's not so much her as who she is."

"I still don't know what you mean."

"Well, look at 'er, look at 'er clobber.   She's got money 'asn't she?   I can't cope with that.   She can speak French an' all.   'ow could I cope with 'er folks, look at me; I can't even speak English."

For the first time I had seen a chink in Albert's armour. He did not have any confidence outside his family unit and his own circle.

"But you're as good as anyone else."

"I can't compete.   What would 'er folks think about me with my crappy clothes and big boots," he said disconsolately.

"But she likes you."

"She feels sorry for me."

"Rubbish.   Why don't you take her out?"

"What with?   Where to?"

Albert was most put out, his first girlfriend and his confidence had gone, but there was an underlying reason and I just realised it at that moment.   Albert was actually ashamed, but before I could put matters right Granddad Heptonstall tugged at my trouser leg from his wheelchair.

"Are you the undertaker?"

"No Mr Heptonstall, I'm the solicitor."

"Well, you've got undertaker's trousers on."

"Yes, but we wear the same pinstripes."

"Getaway, they look smart.   Is it a cremation?"

I realised that Granddad Heptonstall was not completely in control of his faculties but he was a sweet old man who never harmed anyone and I found his eccentricity endearing. He had worked in the steel works for the whole of his working life and his experience had put Jack off work altogether.

"It's not a cremation granddad, I've come to see your son Jack."

"'e's not booking my funeral is 'e?"

"No, granddad," said Albert, "You see fortunately you are not dead yet, so you're OK, OK?"

"I want plenty of flowers."

"Of course you do, I understand," I interjected, trying to placate him.

"Thank you, you are a nice man for an undertaker.   I'm going to be cremated," said the old man forcefully.

"Sooner than you think," interjected Jack, "Stop bothering Mr Smith, 'e 'asn't come 'ere to listen to talk like that."

110

"That's all right Jack, your father and I have been having a chat."

Jack put his arm around his father.

"'e's not a bad old wart, are you father?"

"I'm not bothered about burial," said Mr Heptonstall gravely.

"How are you, Mr Heptonstall?" I asked.

"Eighty four," came the reply. "I'll be eighty five next week. I used to work in the steel works. I've been retired twenty-five years now but I am still fit, I can still walk to the shop and enjoy a pipe of baccy and a brown ale, and I do a bit of gardening, that's why I don't want to be buried, with all the worms and things........."

Jack interrupted.

"Come on now father, you're programme's on T.V. so I'll take you inside and get you a brown ale"

"Thanks son," said the old man holding out his hand toward me.

We shook hands and as he went inside Jack shook his head.

"Silly old bugger," said Jack, "It comes to us all one day."

"I'm going to be cremated," said the old man.

I gave up and tried another avenue.

"Thank you granddad. Have you had something to eat?" I continued.

"Yes, thank you. I'm eighty-four and I've had a cup of tea and a pikelet. But a word of advice..." Granddad paused and looked around as though he didn't want to let anyone hear him speaking, then nodded to me and beckoned me forward to hear him whisper.

"Yes, Granddad?" I whispered.

111

I bent over and placed my ear near to his mouth as he spoke.

"Don't eat the whelks," he said, pointing knowingly to his bottom.

He sat back and nodded. I did not know quite what to say but I was sure he was right.

I smiled and nodded and then I heard someone shout,

"Big Percy's here!"

I turned to see the most enormous man I had ever seen, almost seven feet tall, and I would assume over twenty-five stones, rather like one of the giant American wrestlers. He was wearing tracksuit bottoms and a T-shirt, which accentuated his giant frame. He had black curly hair with the look of a gypsy about him, but his hands were like malt shovels and I later found out that Big Percy was a demolition expert who didn't use explosives or heavy machinery; he just pulled buildings down with his bare hands. The oddest thing of all about him was his rather high-pitched squeaky voice, which did not fit his build at all, and the other remarkable thing was that he was slightly effeminate, although I doubt that anyone would tell him so. I was introduced to him when Jack came back out of the house and Big Percy nearly lifted me off the floor when we shook hands. His wrists and arms were thicker than my own legs. He picked up a tray of chicken legs and munching merrily until thirty at least had been consumed. I watched him eating and when he caught me staring and ambled towards me, I felt disquiet.

"You're the solicitor aren't you?"

"Yes," I said rather apologetically.

"Jack's mate eh?"

"Well, I know him very well, yes."

"E's alreight is Jack."

"Yes, he certainly is."

"Do you want to buy a whippet?"

I was taken aback by the offer, which had not been in context at all with the rest of the conversation.

"No thanks, I've already got a dog."

"Well, if you ever want a good whippet come and see me, I breed 'em. I know all there is to know about whippets."

I nodded in agreement. Big Percy then moved off in search of more food and as he did so it was like the end of an eclipse as the sun came out again when his huge body moved out of the sunlight.

"He's a big bugger Jack," I said.

"Ay, he's big," said Jack, "But e's a nice bloke. 'E'll do some arm-wrestling later on, you'll be able to 'ave a go at 'im. E's never been beaten and e's the cock of Yorkshire. Believe it or not, he drives one of them Harley Davidsons with the big thick tyres on it."

"I thought it would have to have big tyres on it," I replied thoughtfully.

"Yes, it's a fantastic machine, it's the dog's bollocks."

Quite what Big Percy was doing riding up and down on a pair of dog's bollocks was beyond me and it was a description that I had not previously come across, but I was told later that it was a term of endearment, which meant that 'it was the business' or perhaps better, it was an item of unreserved quality.

It was just at that moment I caught sight of Caroline standing alone so I decided to settle my curiosity by engaging her in conversation, since I thought it fascinating that a fine cultured well-spoken and quite beautiful girl would have an interest in somebody like Albert. He just

113

wasn't the ladies' man type, but there could be absolutely no doubt that Caroline actually liked him, so I introduced myself and was surprised to find that she knew of me.

"My father has told me about you, and of course Albert talks about no one else."

"Oh, does he really?" I replied, wondering in what context I had been mentioned.

It wasn't clear to me whether she knew about Albert's chequered past and so I chose my words carefully.

"How did you meet him Caroline?"

"I met him at the animal sanctuary."

"Really?"

"Yes, he's absolutely brilliant with animals and everybody there says he's a genius."

"Oh, he's a genius all right," I said, "I've actually seen him work with animals. I was once at his allotment and I watched him control the geese. It was incredible. I've never seen anybody with such a gift."

"Exactly," said Caroline beaming. "He's so kind and gentle and all the animals respond to him. He is so sweet."

"Oh, he's bloody sweet all right," I thought to myself. "I wonder if she'd like me to tell her about the time when he came to my office and tried to spear my fish!"

"How long have you known him?" I asked.

"Well, I met him first before they went to live up north, but since he's been back he's been going to the animal sanctuary nearly every day. I'm doing a project there for my exams. You see, I want to be a vet."

"That's a very good job indeed. Tell me, what else do you know about him?"

114

"Well, I know he's from a big family and they are all really nice to me, especially his mum, and his dad is a real character isn't he?"

"Oh, he's a real character all right," I said, suppressing a smile.

"I had my tea at their house the other day."

"Did you really?" I asked, "Was it nice?"

"Yes, it was.   I had a lovely time and what a talented family."

"Yes, they certainly are," I replied, resisting the temptation to tell her how they could hot-wire cars and hijack lorries containing electrical goods and cigars.

It was obvious she knew nothing of Albert's criminal past, but I certainly wasn't going to make her any the wiser but as we talked the realisation again came over me as to why Albert was behaving so strangely.   He was ashamed of his past.

"Tell me, what does your father do Caroline?"

I was about to take a drink of punch as she replied.

"He's a Chief Inspector in the police force."

The revelation caused me to choke on the punch which caused me to spray it over the unfortunate Billy One-Leg who had just joined us to complain to the prostrate council official.

"He's in the CID," she continued as I dried my lips with a piece of kitchen roll doubling as a serviette.

"My father is really interested to meet Albert so I intend to take him home with me."

That same choking feeling which came upon me earlier visited me again as my stomach turned with the thought of Albert arriving at a Chief Inspector's house and being questioned concerning his career prospects. I could image how the conversation would go:

"And how do you make your money, Albert?" the Chief Inspector would say.

"By thieving sir, and burglary, and pinching bits off cars, and doing electricity meters. It's not brilliant money, but it's a living!"

And yet for all that I somehow felt protective towards him. It was odd that I could feel disposed towards a villain such as him and I wondered whether I should say something to try to save them both embarrassment, but just then Granddad Heptonstall took my attention again.

As our conversation continued and I took another mouthful of punch to wash down the restriction in my throat but then Albert reappeared in the doorway and I decided to question him about this relationship. Caroline moved away to speak to Madge and I went over to Albert.

"How's things Albert?" I said.

"Alreight Steve. We're glad to be back and more especially we're glad to see thee."

"Thank you Albert," I replied, "And may I say how pleased I am to see you and the rest of the gang."

"Ah, then we're both reight. Have a drink of punch."

I took the glass and looked at the prostrate figure of the Town Hall representative who was murmuring sadly on a rocking-chair, perched precariously at the edge of the pavement.

"As a matter of interest Albert, what is in this punch?"

"Er, rum, brandy, vodka, Southern Comfort and orange juice."

"Really. That accounts for it's kick."

"Not 'alf – you'll know you've 'ad that tomorrow!"

Just then we heard an almighty row.

"Arghhh, bleeding 'ell......Madge.....Madge.....bleeding 'ell........me arse is on fire!"

I recalled Madge's instructions given to Jack earlier. I think he mixed up the pile ointment and the Fiery Jack. Now that's what I call pain!

As time wore on I decided to head back to the office to sign my post. I made my farewells and on my way back reflected on a most unusual afternoon in which I had been offered a whippet dog, told that cremation was better than burial, had tasted Madge's infamous whelk stew, had witnessed a developing love affair between Albert and one of the most beautiful young girls I had ever seen, and had also witnessed a member of the council suffering from alcoholic poisoning, and finally had been called a twat by Billy One-Leg. It was all in a day's work but I couldn't help thinking what fun it would have been to have studied accountancy!

Chapter Seven

'Bye 'Bye Dexter Page

I have been lucky enough to meet a number of characters during my working life, some of whom I have really liked and none more so than the Honourable Sean Page, insurance broker extraordinary.   He had a liking for the high life and a twenty hour working week, but without question he was a 'one off' and with my little world in Yorkshire steadily losing its characters, Pagey has left an indelible mark upon my memory and never more so than at his Uncle Dexter's funeral.

I had been busy looking after the case of Gerry Woodward, who had fallen foul of one of life's great tragedies, namely a broken marriage.   He had one seven year old son called Scott, who was the apple of his eye but unfortunately owing to an acrimonious divorce there were problems with access.   It was one of those side effects which often occur in matrimonial cases when the children become pawns in the game of 'getting even with my spouse'.

At the end of the day I suppose it was a case of six of one and half a dozen of the other, but Gerry was a very good father and whilst he loved Norma his former wife, they simply could not get on.   An aggravating feature was that Norma was an alcoholic and regrettably Gerry was going the same way.   He had had a good education at University where he had earned a degree and had just started work in the field of computers.

His wife refused to let him see his son and so Gerry had been to see me, with a view to pursuing a case for access; something easier said than done.

Unfortunately Norma had chosen to be awkward so we had been left with no alternative but to fight it out in the courts where Gerry had won the case and been awarded what was called 'specified access' which meant that he saw his son at certain times on certain days. I had been told that there was the prospect of a reconciliation but then Norma tragically contracted cancer of the liver. Fortunately for her she did not suffer for long, and she died during the early part of that year.

Gerry had begun his own decline into drink and the Social Services had become involved because they felt that Gerry's rather inadequate one roomed flat was unsuitable to bring up a young child, thereby justifying their intervention.

There was a hearing before the Magistrates to determine whether the child should be taken into care and I had had a meeting with Gerry to try to sort out some reasonable accommodation, which would help our case. Unfortunately his behaviour proved unacceptable and in terms of his case against the local authority he was playing into their hands. His course of self-destruction was to have a great effect, not only upon himself but also on his son Scott, yet it seemed as if he was powerless to do anything about it even though he could see what was happening.

On this particular visit he was drunk and he seemed to be having great difficulty coming to terms with his wife's death, as well as dealing with the whole issue of the care of his son.

The meeting had to be suspended owing to Gerry's condition and I was busily trying to pick up the threads of his application when Pagey telephoned.

"Now then old bean, what's the state of play eh?"

"Not too bad Pagey old son. I've got plenty on but I'm not complaining."

"Had a spot of bad news old bean," said Pagey in an otherwise bright-sounding tone.

"Uncle Dexter snuffed it old bean."

"Oh, I'm sorry to hear that Pagey. You got on with him quite well didn't you?"

"Certainly did old man, he was a great sport, a fine boozer and a gentleman. The trouble and strife doted on him. She's very upset."

"Yes, I can imagine she would be," I said sympathetically. "What a nice chap he was."

"Well I'm ringing you old bean to tell you that the funeral is tomorrow before which old Dexter's lying in state at my house for people to come and pay their respects. The funeral is at 3 o'clock, the hearse is arriving at 2.15 to take him away to have the flowers put on the coffin, and then they'll come back when everybody else arrives at 2.45. Then off to the church and the crem."

Pagey's matter of fact way of describing the forthcoming events was consistent with his nature. There was absolutely no doubt he was moved by the loss of his uncle, but duty had to be done and he was the one to sort out the arrangements.

"Are you coming for a pre-cremation swig?"

"Yes," I replied, "I'll do that. What time do you want me there?"

"Oh," said Pagey, "Get here about quarter to two and then we've half an hour before the old stiff's taken away."

"Very good I replied, I'll see you then."

120

My case the following afternoon had been cancelled because the Defendant had sent in a sick-note which confirmed bleeding haemorrhoids and so I wasn't needed at the court that afternoon.

I knew Dexter, having attended one or two of the great boozing sessions that he and Pagey indulged in and it was fitting that I should pay my respects.

He was an incredible character, in his seventies, but still with a full head of hair although it had turned white. He was very distinguished and wore expensive suits which gave him the air of a medical man, although his business had been based in the buying and selling of land. He had enjoyed a long life of bachelordom and although he had had a succession of close girlfriends he managed to avoid the altar with all of them.

He had some other relatives who had little or no contact with him, but I understood that they had been invited to the funeral and would be attending from their various homes in the south of England. I understood that they were Methodists and as such did not particularly approve of the taking of alcohol. They had all taken the view that Sean was following in his uncle's footsteps and as such was past redemption, despite the fact that he had done his very best on their rather rare meetings to come over as a well-meaning and responsible adult.

I set off from the office just after the close of the morning court, arriving at approximately 1.15pm. Pagey was host to Lewis Frame, the mad Scotsman and the great Jarvis, who had arrived just before me and were partaking of copious quantities of Newcastle Brown Ale backed up with the odd spot of brandy. I had realised the possibilities of this meeting and like my colleagues had made use of the local taxi firm run by a friend and client Geoff Taylor.

I was given two drinks and after the usual salutations were exchanged Pagey invited us all into the front room to pay our last respects. It was a rather disquieting experience, for there was Dexter with his arms folded looking serene set against the white satin-backed coffin whilst Pagey urged his reluctant visitors forward for a 'peek at the stiff'.

"Not a bad looking old stick was he, even now? It's a shame he missed my birthday, we were in for a really big session, but the poor old bugger hasn't made it."

The poor old bugger, as Pagey described him, hadn't made the birthday but he'd made just about every other party that had been arranged in our group, and whilst he'd had a long and glorious life, it was nevertheless a moving moment to witness the demise of such a great character.

Pagey waxed lyrical in his inimitable manner about various stories from Dexter's past and then he administered drinks to us all and we honoured Dexter with a toast.

"Here's to old Dexter, entrepreneur, first division boozer and all round good egg."

Pagey took a giant swig from a pint of Newcastle Brown and whilst we all muttered our support to the Toast, Pagey put his glass down on the corner of the coffin.

"He'd be pleased that you lot have turned up," said Pagey proudly. "It should be a real good send-off for the old salt – God bless you Dexter, old man," he said as he gesticulated towards the deceased's head with his hand.

Unfortunately he had forgotten that the pint was perched precariously on the corner of the coffin and inevitably there was contact!

The pint glass fell into the coffin and covered the top of the shroud and satin lining, and regrettably poor old Dexter's shock of white hair was covered in Newcastle Brown ale. We all gasped. Pagey uttered some extremely vulgar and inappropriate remarks and issued forth those immortal words,

"Now what are you going to do?"

The rest of the group looked at each other and before the very first letter 'F' was spoken, Pagey put his head in his hands. This deterred any outburst of criticism and we all gathered round the coffin to see the damage. Newcastle Brown is a gloriously dark beer and not surprisingly, when it comes into contact with satin it leaves a substantial stain. In addition, it smells and when poured across human hair, has the effect of darkening the subject matter and making it incredibly sticky.

By this time it was ten past two and the funeral directors were due at quarter past, although the guests were not due until quarter to three. We were all in a quandary as to know what to do for the best because as Dexter's family and friends would file past the coffin prior to it being closed, they wouldn't be too impressed at seeing a beer-swilled shroud and soaking wet hair. Whilst Dexter liked a drink, we doubted very much if we could convince anybody that he'd had one last pint before the cremation and as Pagey's concern got worse, the master stroke came to him.

"I know," said Pagey, "If we can dry Dexter's hair and the satin, we can chuck some talcum powder about which might cover up the discoloration. The old expression 'it seemed a good idea at the time' was never more appropriate than in that situation and Pagey disappeared upstairs returning within seconds with a very large hairdryer and a tin of pungent smelling powder used for treating athletes foot.

"Lift his head up while I dry the back of his hair," said Pagey.

"Bugger off," I retorted, seeing that he was looking at me.

"Come on, Smithy," said Pagey, "Be a sport."

"Be a sport? Be a sport? You must think I fell out of a tree. I'm not lifting his head up, ask Jarvis to do it."

"Sod off," said Jarvis, "I'm not doing it."

"Oh, come on," said Pagey, "This is ridiculous. You can't leave me to swing for this, they'll be here in a minute."

"Come here," said Bodger, "I'll do it."

"Well done old bean," said Pagey, "Gently there. Smithy, come on just put this satin straight, and you do the other side Jarvis."

With great reluctance Jarvis and I walked towards the coffin and pulled tight the satin, whilst Pagey began drying out the cloth.

"His head's cold," said Bodger.

"Brilliant! It would be, he's dead isn't he?" I replied sarcastically.

"Bloody hell," said Pagey, "It's taking ages for this to dry."

"Pagey did his best with the satin and Bodger began administering the talcum powder to it, smoothing it out carefully to remove the beer marks. Pagey then started enthusiastically drying Dexter's hair with considerable panache.

The scene can only be imagined in one's wildest dreams. Bodger was holding Dexter's head up, I was supporting his left shoulder and Jarvis his right. There was Pagey making a considerable mess of drying the beer-anointed scalp. In our frenzy we hadn't realised or heard the arrival of the undertaker, or more importantly of Dexter's Methodist relatives, including the fearsome Auntie Margaret, from the Hitler Youth. The door sprang open and Auntie Margaret was in mid sentence.

"Sean, it's Aunt Margaret and Uncle Jeffrey. We've arrived with the undertaker early so as to be able to pay our respects to ………."

Just at that moment Auntie Margaret, Uncle Jeffrey and the undertaker and his staff entered the room and caught sight of our distinguished group. There we were as if paralysed by fear, staring back at them who in turn were staring back at us open-mouthed. The silence seemed to last for ages, until it was broken by Pagey speaking quickly and very nervously.

"Uncle Margaret and Auntie Jeffrey, how wonderful to see you again. Come in and say hello to Uncle Dexter, we were just er……drying his hair."

Unfortunately during this speech Pagey had forgotten to switch off the hairdryer which had caused poor old Dexter's hair to stand up on end, almost as if he had suffered some tremendous shock, but then again I suppose he had!

Chapter Eight

Mrs Mott's Illness and Gerry Loses Round One

It was the morning after the night before when I was suffering from the effects of one of our monthly soirées. Pagey had been down in the dumps, having been completely ostracised by the Methodist branch of his family and poor old Dexter had had his hair dried for the last time. The Wake had ended in complete chaos as Pagey and the Three Musketeers had been barred from the funeral tea.

The Thursday morning saw me arrive at the office late and attempt to go through a stream of correspondence before setting out to deal with the morning's court. Mrs Mott, our remarkable cleaner, had spotted that I had something of a hangover. Quite how she had worked it out was a wonder to me, but then on reflection the fact that I had heavy bags under my eyes, I was moaning pathetically, was wearing dark glasses, stank like a brewery and was drinking from a jug full of water probably gave her a clue.

"You look under the weather Mr Smith," said Mrs Mott sympathetically.

"I've just got a bit of a headache Mrs Mott. I'm afraid I had one over the eight last night."

"More like eight over the eight," said Mrs Mott. "Anyway look, I'll fetch you some Alza Seltzer and drink it straight down. I'll then give you a spoonful of honey in some vinegar – it's the best remedy in the world."

"It's the best remedy for making you sick I thought to myself, but Mrs Mott meant well and I had no wish to offend her.

I sampled the two concoctions, the latter making me wince so much that I screwed my face up sufficiently to challenge the National Gurning Champion.

"Not very nice is it?" said Mrs Mott as though inflicting dreadful pain would outweigh the feeling of dehydration.

"All you've got to do now Mr Smith is to keep that down. It'll cure it in an hour although it might make you a bit loose."

"A bit loose?" I queried.

"Ay," said Mrs Mott, "It might make you run a bit."

"It might make me run a lot," I replied as I could not remove the vile taste from my palate.

"Don't drink any water while that vinegar settles," said Mrs Mott.

"Yes, but it's the after-taste in my mouth Mrs Mott," I said pathetically.

"You'll have to put up with that. You'll know not to do it next time."

Medical practice according to Doctor Mott did not meet with my complete enthusiasm, but who was I to argue? I gathered my papers together and left for court.

"You look rough," said Tracey, who was standing in reception resplendent in a suede suit in the latest designer style.

"Thank you Tracey, you've made my day," I replied and woefully trudged off down the stairs. As I left the entrance I saw Gerry Woodward waiting in the doorway and noticed that he had three days' growth of beard, his hair was totally unkempt and he reeked as though he had slept in a brewery. In fact he looked very similar to me.

"Now then Gerry, what's the problem?" I asked.

"It's not good Steve," he said, speaking in a gravel-tone voice. "I saw Social Services last night and they are going for an interim care order. They seem to think that the court will grant it.

"Well if they do," I replied, "The order only lasts for twenty-eight days and then it's got to be renewed, that will give you a month to get your act together."

"How the bloody 'ell can I do that? Just look at the state of me. I've nowhere for 'im to live, I'm pissed every day and quite frankly I'm losing the will."

It's always the case that something urgent and massively important to someone happens when you are in a rush.

"Look Gerry, I'm late for court as it is, but if you would like to come up there with me, when we get a break I'll buy you a cup of tea and we'll have a chat."

"OK," said Gerry, "I'll walk up to court with you."

The poor tormented man had not only lost his job, his home and his wife but was about to lose the only thing he had left, his son, and there was I suffering a bigger hangover than him trying to advise him to stay off the drink. At least I was only a part hypocrite because my boozing activities were restricted to only two or three days a week, whereas Gerry seemed to have time for nothing else.

I went into court having had six cases to deal with that day, representing a variety of sins including shoplifters, carlifters and shirtlifters with a couple of prostitutes thrown in for good measure.

One of the girls laid claim to be called Veronique LaTour but according to her criminal record her real name was Mavis Juppe, who had been born near Grimsby and had a list of convictions which extended to about ten pages for minor theft and prostitution. She had been 'on the game' since her mid-teens and whilst the record said that she was thirty years of age, she looked considerably older. Her co-accused was another lady of the night, an old client we have met before and one who gloried in the golden name of FiFi DuPont, alias Janet Wadkin.

They had been picked up by the police wandering up and down the street outside the local nightclub and had been charged with soliciting but they were pleading not guilty on the basis that they were merely walking up and down outside the nightclub, waiting for their boyfriends to pick them up. They had walked in opposite directions to ensure that they were able to cover the two directions from where these young men could arrive, but the evidence was that they were seen to be walking up and down the street outside the nightclub, speaking to a number of young males, allegedly offering their services. They were arrested, their bags were searched and each was found to contain a strange electrical appliance together with various packets of condoms.

The Defendants on the other hand were saying that they were speaking to various men, simply asking after their boyfriends and they always carried condoms to cover all eventualities. The difficulty was that they looked like prostitutes and when they were due to give their evidence I feared that they would even sound like them.

I took them into the rat hole interview room to discuss the case further and we went through the evidence together; I was not impressed with their story and suggested that perhaps a court might find it difficult to believe their version of events.

"Are you trying to say that we look guilty," said Veronique in a broad South Yorkshire accent, without even a hint of French.

"It's not that," I said apologetically, "The court will look at all the surrounding evidence and they will put two and two together and I think they will make four."

"Well they ought to be shot with shit," said Miss DuPont.

"True," I said, "But that still doesn't get us out of this particular difficulty, even if they were so shot."

"We still want to fight it Steve," said Veronique, "Besides, there's nothing wrong with carrying a few Johnny's is there?"

"Of course not" I said, trying to placate the rising tide of distrust which was beginning to come between us.

"So that's it then," said FiFi, "We're both not guilty, sod 'em!"

There was no real answer to that comment and I doubted whether the Magistrates would be interested in that possibility so I just nodded my head in agreement and we marched into court, where I was greeted by Keith Copley the Court Clerk.

"What have you got for us today, Steve?" he asked.

"I have got three pleas, two adjournments, and Miss LaTour and Miss DuPont who insist that they are pleading not guilty to soliciting."

"The court won't like that," said Keith Copley.

Veronique's final words in our conversation came to mind, but modesty forbade me to reiterate them to Keith.

"Do you want to call them first?" asked Keith.

130

"No, I'll not bother, they're outside drumming up a bit of trade. I'll get rid of my other adjournments first if I may?"

"As you please," said Copley just as the three Magistrates walked into court; one of them being known locally as the 'Lord Chief Justice' and with whom I had crossed swords so many times in the past. He had been at the Magistrates' Court meeting where the then Lord Chancellor's letter had been read out to them saying that there were too many adjournments which was causing massive delays in the legal system and increasing the Legal Aid bill. The result was inevitable, he was going to refuse any applications to adjourn, particularly if I was for the defence.

Despite the fact that my friend Neil Franklin of the Crown Prosecution Service raised no objection to my three adjournments (for indeed they were necessary for proper legal reasons), the 'Lord Chief Justice' tried to complicate things for me by refusing the applications, and Keith Copley had to intervene on my behalf to point out that the adjournments were not actually for my benefit, but more in the interests of justice.

It was clear that the 'Lord Chief Justice' was annoyed at having to adjourn the cases, and seemed to think for some weird reason peculiar to him that it was all my fault. I realised that in the retirement room he would be telling his colleagues that 'Steve Smith was always asking for adjournments', but that's the way it was, and always will be in court life. He disliked me and he was going to do everything in his power to cause me problems.

We then called Mesdames LaTour and DuPont into the courtroom, where FiFi gave her address, date of birth, lied about both and was followed by Veronique.

"What is your full name please?"

"Veronique Maisy LaTour, name changed by deed poll."

"Very good," said Keith, "And your address please Madam?"

"42 Loughborough Rise, Wath, and I'm in most evenings after 11pm."

The observers in the public gallery burst into laughter whereas Keith pretended to miss the point entirely and asked her date of birth.

"A gentleman shouldn't ask a lady her date of birth," said Veronique.

"Oh, get on with it," said the 'Lord Chief Justice', "You are charged with an offence and you are obliged to answer the court's questions."

"I may be charged with an offence," said Veronique indignantly, "But as I have not yet been convicted I believe that this court must treat me as an innocent person, and whilst you may have no respect for me, the very least you can do is to show a sense of respect for the court and the people's rights."

"Well said," I thought to myself.

The 'Lord Chief Justice' coughed and spluttered

"Will you speak to your client Mr Smith?"

"What about sir?" I asked, deliberately evading the point.

"Her conduct Mr Smith, her conduct, and watch your own whilst you do it."

"Watch my own whilst I do what?" I asked myself.

I spoke to Veronique who giggled incessantly as though I had told her a joke.   The 'Lord Chief Justice' grunted at me and shouted,

"MR SMITH!!"

"Yes Sir?"

"Are you quite ready?"

"Yes sir, thank you, quite ready."

"Well get on with it."

I resisted the temptation to tell him to drop dead.

The 'Lord Chief Justice' um'd and ah'd before inviting Keith to take the Defendants' pleas.

"Not guilty plea," said FiFi

"Not guilty plea, most certainly," said Veronique.

The 'Lord Chief Justice' asked if we could proceed there and then but Keith Copley had to tell him that the witnesses wouldn't be present and there would have to be an adjournment to enable the police to bring them to court.

I could not resist my next comment.

"May it please you sir, I am in a position to proceed today, but if the court requires an adjournment I won't object." I smiled as I sat down and the 'Lord Chief' coughed and spluttered even more. My attention was drawn by a tap on my shoulder and when I turned, Veronique said in a stage whisper,

"That's put one up him."

"Yes, I rather think it has," I replied.

Keith Copley winked at me and I bowed graciously before leaving the court. As I walked out of the double doors into the court corridor Veronique nipped my bottom quite firmly and announced for all to hear that I had a 'nice arse'. The 'Lord Chief Justice' did not say a word, but then I suspected that he hadn't got a nice arse.

I took Gerry for a cup of tea in the WRVS tea-room, fought my way through the smoke and smog from the aftermath of a hundred cigarettes and then we made our way to the rat hole interview room. On the way I was offered a Rolex watch, a tube of Ganger (Marijuana), an evening out with a young woman who appeared to have one leg and finally one of the latest hairdryers, which not long ago would have suited Pagey down to the ground. My experience however had taught me never to buy anything from the many unsavoury characters at court as the inevitability was that it was nicked.

I politely declined the generous offers and then I was approached by Veronique who embarrassed me by putting a contraceptive in my top pocket and saying that I should save it for later and she would give me a ring and 'fix a date'. I beat a hasty retreat to the solicitors' room to recount the story to some of the other solicitors, where a young man called Julian Tierney, the son of my former mentor and employer George Tierney, was working in the court for his father. He had heard the reference to the contraceptive and found it amusing, so I threw it at him in jest, then left the solicitors' room to go back into court to deal with my other cases. I was therefore blissfully unaware that Tierney had opened the contraceptive, unrolled it and placed it in the pocket of my mackintosh. When I returned to the room Julian had disappeared, but as I put on my coat and placed my hands into my pockets to retrieve my keys, I was stopped in my tracks by the realisation of something oily and soft coming into contact with the palm of my hand.

"You bastard," I said to myself as I drew out the contraceptive from my pocket just as a WRVS lady entered the solicitors' room to collect cups. She caught sight of me holding the offending item, when understandably she cleared her throat with a pronounced cough, collected the cups and left tutting.

"Bloody marvellous!" I thought to myself, this will be the talk of the tea-room and such a story would travel like wildfire, so whether anyone believed it or not that old Rotherham maxim: 'if you throw enough shit about everyone will get a bit' would apply, ensuring that henceforth I would be known as the 'Johnny-Toting Brief'. The least I could do was to return the compliment so I put the rubber into Julian's coat pocket or so I thought.

I was telling my friend David Walters, a solicitor and colleague the story when in walked Julian. We said nothing as Julian picked up his coat, smiled, bade farewell and left without noticing anything, but immediately there was a major problem; Julian had not picked up the coat with the contraceptive. However before I got a chance to move, a visiting Magistrate from Sheffield came in to collect the potentially embarrassing garment and we watched in horror as he put it on.

To make matters worse he was joined by the chairman of the Magistrates' Court, the chairman's wife and the 'Lord Chief Justice', who sneered at me as he walked in, in the company of dignitaries, who looked as though they were fresh out of the Methodist mission. The immortal words, 'oh shite' came to mind as I inched towards the door in the certain knowledge that I ought to make myself scarce.

Just as I got to the door the Chairman of the Magistrates announced that he had found the meeting at Rotherham most stimulating and would have liked to have stayed longer, but he had another appointment elsewhere. He then reached into his coat pocket for his car keys and everyone stood in silence.

"I should like to take this opportunity of thanking everyone at Rotherham Magistrates Court for their hospitality, so much so that I think I had better hand my car keys to my wife so that she can drive.   I wouldn't want to be breathalysed."

Everyone laughed out of courtesy.

"Here are the keys dear…….."

The gathering stood in open-mouthed silence as the Magistrate handed over to his wife a set of car keys which sadly had an unfurled condom attached to them.   It was almost as if we were watching in slow motion as the unfortunate lady accepted the keys and the other unwanted item before they quietly and rather unsteadily left the room, exchanging glances with a mortified audience.   For some reason they were unable to speak.

"Cheerio then," I said brightly and took my leave as the deputation remained in the room almost riveted to the spot with shock.   As I got outside the worst thing that could have happened, did happen; Veronique La Tour and Miss DuPont caught sight of the Chairman of the Magistrates, who meanwhile had thought it more chivalrous to retrieve his keys from his wife and now seemed so stunned as to walk with them, still having the condom attached, down the length of the corridor.

"I'm glad to see you've brought your own," said Veronique.   "Twenty quid to you, you look like a good sport! I like a man that brings his own."

The Magistrate did not answer and then some wag shouted, "I'll borrow that after you!"

Gerry was waiting for me outside the court, drinking from a can of lager which I took out of his hand and put on the ledge, before taking him outside.

"That is no way to face a crisis," I said.

"I'm sorry Steve, but I just needed a livener."

"Suppose someone from Social Services saw you doing that, then it's game set and match isn't it?   You know what they are like."

"I suppose so, but I've got nothing left to fight with."

"Well you just can't give up, that's ridiculous.   Does that kid mean anything to you at all?"

"Of course he does," replied Gerry angrily, "But I just don't seem to be able to get my act together without a drink."

"If you take my advice you'll leave the drink well alone and you'll start acting like a responsible parent."

I noticed Gerry's eyes begin to redden and moisten and he turned away as tears streamed down his cheeks.

I put an arm around the disconsolate man and guided him out of the court building back towards the office.

Three weeks later I went into the office and made myself ready to appear at court to answer the application for an interim care order.   Gerry turned up unshaven dishevelled and reeking of alcohol.   Scott, his child, wasn't present and the Social Services went through the motions of presenting the case as strongly as they could in favour of taking the child away.   I have to admit that I was somewhat resentful, because it seemed as though the local authority were treating this purely as a personal contest as they so desperately applied themselves to countering each of my arguments.   It did seem that the case was more about beating us than anything else; but beat us they did.

The Chairman of the Magistrates was from an upper middle-class background, who having sent his own son to public school was now steering him through University. He had had sufficient finance to retire early and now lived a very good life in one of the more expensive suburbs of

Rotherham.   He was a fair man and I had no complaints about his judgement, but he had never really been able to see how the other half lived, so that not unreasonably he was appalled at the catalogue of material which the Social Services had thrown at us.   He spoke slowly and deliberately when informing the court that the Magistrates had come to the conclusion that in the best interests of the child there had to be an interim care order.   The child would be placed in the care of the local authority at an address designated by them and over the next four weeks full information would be placed before the court to see what steps had been taken to rectify or improve the situation.

It was almost as if an olive branch had been offered to Gerry by saying that the court would be interested to see what steps he had taken in the intervening period to resolve his difficulties.

Whilst it was heart-breaking for Gerry he had left the court with little option, and even though the result was entirely his own fault I couldn't help feeling sorry for a man whose life had taken such a dramatic turn downward.

By the time I got out of court Gerry had gone and I wandered down to the Cross Keys, where sure enough my instinct proved right; there he was sitting at the bar drinking a pint of lager with a double brandy.   He was disconsolate and I saw little point in continuing our conversation.

I returned to the office and was surprised to see Mrs Mott busy polishing my desk.   She didn't usually appear at work until after the office had closed, but for some reason she had appeared early.

"You're in early Mrs Mott," I said.

"Yes Mr Smith," she said, "I wanted to … get … I wanted to ….. It's not my fault. I don't know how to tell you this, but……."

She looked and indeed she was very upset so I asked her to sit down and offered her a drink.

"Would you like something to drink?" I asked her.

"Oh, that would be very nice."

Before I got the chance to order a cup of tea she asked for a large whisky. I looked up to the ceiling, went to the cabinet to pour it out and gave it to her. It was then that she delivered the bombshell.

"I've been to the hospital Mr Smith and they've told me I'm not very well 'down there'."

"Down where?" I asked naively.

"You know, women's problems."

"Oh dear, I am sorry to hear that Mrs Mott." I said. "Is there anything I can do?"

"It's not that," said Mrs Mott, "You see, it's not very good…….. I'm not going to be able to…….."

"Whatever is the matter Mrs Mott?" I asked anxiously.

"I've got cancer Mr Smith," she said. "And its in an advanced stage. I've been poorly for some time but I thought it was just a bit of old age. Unfortunately it's not and the hospital say that I've got to have chemotherapy."

I was shocked and at first I couldn't think of anything to say.

"I am sure they will be able to rectify the problem, won't they?"

Mrs Mott looked at the floor and didn't reply.

I didn't need any other clues and I was desperately trying to think of something sensible to say.

"They don't know at home," she said, "And I don't quite know how to tell them, but I'm going to have the treatment just the same, as you never know there may be a chance."

"There's always a chance Mrs Mott," I said placing my arm around her shoulders. "When does this treatment start?"

"On Monday," she said.

"That's quick. At least there'll be some progress."

She attempted a smile before speaking.

"I've got my sister to stand in for me," she said. "She goes on a bit, but she's honest and she's a good sort. If you'll allow it, she'll take over."

"She will take over until you come back," I said confidently.

"Well, I also have to have an operation, so the doctor seems to think that I'll have to retire."

I didn't want to broach the subject because it seemed to upset her and it certainly upset me, so I tried everything in my power to get her off the subject.

"Let's see what happens Mrs Mott. I think you'll be OK. You look too well to me!"

I was lying, because she didn't look well at all and if I had only taken the time and trouble to look at her more carefully, I would have noticed a general deterioration in her complexion and overall demeanour.

"You're good men you and Mr Wilford, you're both gentlemen. That's why everybody likes you. You've been so very good to me, I can't bear the thought of letting you down."

Here was a woman facing the biggest struggle of her life, and all she could think about was letting her employer down. I was almost moved to tears by her thoughtfulness.

"I'll finish tomorrow then, if I may and I'll bring Vera in with me, to show her the ropes."

"We'll all come and visit you Mrs Mott," I said, "And I'm sure that you will be OK."

She smiled, kissed me on the cheek and then turned and walked out of the room.

"I know you'll be OK," I shouted after her, but she was gone.

It had been a bloody awful day, full of bad news and trauma and there was I, helpless and hopeless, in my fumbled attempts to try to reassure an ageing lady whose only fault in life was to grow old.

The following day saw Mrs Mott arrive at the office bright and early so by the time I arrived the whole room was spick and span, as usual. A rather large lady of senior years greeted me at the top of the stairs, who I estimated would be in her late sixties. She had grey hair combed back which was tied in a bun at the back of her head, and was just over five feet tall but fat. She had the same emerald green eyes as her sister, Mrs Mott, was possessed of a pleasant honest face, worn by the rigours of life, and was wearing a multi-coloured pinafore. However the most noticeable part of her apparel was a pair of blue fur-rimmed carpet slippers, which she caught me looking at out of the corner of her eye.

"Hello Mr Smith, bunions," she said, pointing to her feet, "I'm Vera, Mrs Mott's sister. I am pleased to meet you."

We shook hands and I was immediately amazed by the force of her grip. Mrs Mott then walked into the room.

"I see you've introduced yourself Vera."

"Ay," said Vera, "You're right, he's not bad looking, although he could do with a haircut and losing a bit of weight."

"Oh God," I thought, concealing a smile, "She's just like her sister!"

As Mrs Mott was about to leave, all the staff gathered together so that we could make a presentation. We had bought her a television and video and a large bouquet of flowers.

She was overcome by emotion and having made her excuses she left. We would miss her greatly and even Wilf had to clear his throat to remove the lump.

"I've got some mixture for your acid Mr Smith. My sister told me you suffer a lot with wind."

"Not really Vera, I had acid but not wind…."

She was undeterred.

"Come on, medicine in, wind out!"

Wilf laughed and left.

"That's done it. It would be the talk of the Cross Keys now, Smithy and his wind, bloody marvellous; Mrs Mott had struck again!

Despite my protests I downed the medicine in one with the effect that I was convinced I had been poisoned. I could not help but say under my breath,

"Come back Mrs Mott, all is forgiven."

It was an average week without anything particularly outstanding and each day I checked with Vera about her sister, to be told that 'no news was good news' until the Friday of the following week when Vera was less chirpy than usual so I asked her if she had any news.

"How are things Vera?"

"Not too good. Alice has got to have an operation on Monday. They have decided there's no alternative.

"Oh no," I replied. "What else has the doctor said?"

Vera took her time repeating what she had been told. She stammered as she spoke, clearly upset at her sister's plight.

"They don't know if they've caught it in time, but one thing's for sure, if she doesn't have this operation the cancer will spread. They told her that but for the operation she would only have six months left."

I shook my head in disbelief.

"I'm sorry to have mentioned it now Vera. Is there anything I can do?

"Nothing thank you Mr Smith. By the way, she thanks you for the card and the flowers that you sent."

"Oh, that's all right," I said, "It was the very least we could do. If there's anything else, I will be delighted to help."

Vera smiled and shook her head and as she was leaving my room to go about her work an idea came to her and she turned.

"Well, there is one thing Mr Smith," she said, "If you could that is..........."

"Just name it Vera. I'll do whatever I can."

"It would be nice if you could pop to see her before the operation."

"I'd be delighted to. The only reason I've not visited before is that I understand it's only two visitors per person and I didn't want to get in the way of the family."

"No, that's all right Mr Smith, she would be thrilled to bits to see you."

"Well, I'm covering the court on Saturday morning and I'll go at lunchtime if that's OK?"

143

"Yes, they won't mind you going in to see her then. I think she will be really pleased. She might appear a bit groggy but that's because of all the drugs they are giving her."

"I understand," I replied. "Please tell her I'll call and see her on Saturday.

"That's smashing," she said wiping a tear from her face as she went about her business.

Saturday came soon enough and I headed off to a hospital in Sheffield, where on reaching the ward I wanted, because I was not exactly within visiting time I went to wait at the Sister's office to see if it was in order for me to see her. The Sister, a very rotund lady, with bright red hair and a vivacious smile, had a kind face which lit up when she smiled. I explained the position and she told me that I was expected, taking me to a room which Mrs Mott shared with five other ladies.

I went inside to find Mrs Mott in a corner by the window. She was pleased to see me, as I was to see her, although by now looking very tired and grey of complexion. Her beautiful emerald-coloured eyes lit up as she spoke and as she sat up in bed she winced with pain, which flashed across her eyes like a beacon.

"It seems like a silly question Mrs Mott, but how are you?"

"I'm all right Mr Smith. I'm in a bit of discomfort but it's not too bad. I suppose it's the waiting really which gets you down most. I've made some good friends in here, some nice people. That's Mrs Essex over there, she's got the same problem as me and the lady at the far end, Mrs Broughton, lives not far from us, so I've got plenty of company and they are all nice ladies."

"Have the family been to see you?"

Yes, they come twice a day and they stay all day on Saturdays and Sundays. They're a good set, they really are. Our Vera pops in after work. She's settling down really well and she's having a marvellous time."

"She's doing very well indeed, we're very happy with her, but there's only one Mrs Mott."

Her eyes moistened and she placed her hand on mine, squeezing it.

"Thanks ever so much for coming to see me," she said, "It's so nice of you."

"Oh that reminds me, I've brought you some Turkish Delight. Your Vera says it's your favourite."

"Oh, that's nice of you."

"Steve Wilford's coming to see you tomorrow. He says he going to bring you a bottle of Guinness."

"Well, he'll have to sneak it in, as they're very strict here about alcohol."

We both laughed and then the nurse came into the ward and told me that she needed to carry out some tests and so I prepared to leave.

I stood up and as I was walking out I tried to offer some words of encouragement.

"Don't forget Mrs Mott, when this operation is done I want you back in that office as soon as you're recovered."

She smiled, waved and nodded and I couldn't help thinking what a tremendously brave woman she was.

On my way out I called at the Sister's office and thanked her for allowing the visit out of visiting hours but the real reason was to ask about Mrs Mott's condition.

"What are the chances of the operation being a success Sister, if I may ask?"

She gave me the stock standard answer which was really all I could expect and indeed all I was entitled to,

"It's not clear how far the cancer has gone but we'll know more after the operation. The surgeon is very good and very experienced and I have every faith in him."

It was surprising what the effect of those words of encouragement was.

Wilf went to see Mrs Mott on the Sunday and I understand he took her a bottle of Guinness, which was placed in her tiny locker at the side of the bed. She was not allowed to drink it prior to the operation but it was the thought that mattered.

Vera didn't work on the Monday or Tuesday because she had a great deal of running about to do looking after her family and standing on call for the hospital. She rang me on Tuesday morning to tell me that the operation had taken place and early indications were good. Mrs Mott was comfortable but the effects of the drugs and anaesthetic caused her to sleep most of the time so it would be some days before she was fit to receive visitors other than her family.

The following morning I received a telephone call from the police to say that one of my drug addict clients had committed suicide whilst on remand at the prison and there was Mrs Mott in hospital, fighting for her life. Somehow it just didn't seem fair.

Chapter Nine

Whatever Happened to Gerry's Kid?

The next few weeks saw a remarkable change in Gerry Woodward's attitude and whilst he had not completely given up alcohol he had cut down to less than a third of his normal intake.   He had smartened himself up, wore fresh clean clothes every day, made sure his hair was always well-groomed and he shaved regularly.   He had signed on at the local technical college for a re-training course in computers which he was attending each week-day without default and was seeing his son regularly at the foster home. Gerry had worked hard and I was moved to see such effort without any outside assistance, because our campaign to see the return of his son was gathering momentum, although one of our main problems was his self-imposed alienation from Miss Stackpole, the Social Worker who had been assigned to the case.   Miss Stackpole was a lady of some fifty years, a spinster of whom it was said, was possessed of considerable experience in dealing with children.   She was the epitome of the left-wing assertive female having a short hairstyle with a clearly defined parting but perversely the crown of her head had a tuft of hair, which resisted entirely any attempt to flatten it.   She looked a formidable woman of heavy build, who wore sturdy walking shoes and a tweed suit enhanced by a necklace of dress pearls.   She had a habit of peering over her half-moon spectacles with a look of complete distrust and unfortunately Gerry's relationship with her had got off on the wrong foot, so that she had already formed a dislike of him. To say we were up against it was an understatement but he was doing his best.

The case had been adjourned for a full formal hearing which meant that reports of all manner and description would be prepared by social workers and these would centre upon the interests of the child, which of course were quite properly paramount.

Whilst I had grave concerns prior to Gerry's rehabilitation, I had certainly become more hopeful as his attitude and conduct improved.

I suppose the catalyst for this was one particular visit, which was quite upsetting, when I had gone along to check on Scott's circumstances to make sure he was being properly cared for. He was with a very nice family who had fostered many children in the past, and their caring attitude had given them a considerable insight into the plight of young people caught up in such difficulties, so that fortunately they could see Gerry's point of view as well, which was another step in the right direction as far as we were concerned.

One night at their home Scott was sitting watching television when Gerry and I turned up to visit him and we were shown every courtesy despite the fact that the family were mid-way through preparing the evening meal, so no doubt could well have done without us.

As I was talking to the foster parents I left Gerry with his son for ten minutes or so and when we all returned to the lounge we saw Gerry and Scott hugging each other – both in tears. We heard Gerry promising him that he would get him home which seemed to be the only way he could be placated and I was pleased that the foster parents had actually witnessed this, for such outbursts of emotion cannot be orchestrated and I was sure the incident could become a useful part of my case.

One of Gerry's difficulties had been housing but one day he came into the office bubbling over with excitement to report that he had been to see a private landlord and had acquired a small terraced house in a suburb of Rotherham. There was a tiny garden area at the front, augmented by a much larger garden with a shed at the rear, and the house needed to be decorated but otherwise it was wind and watertight.

Over the next two to three weeks Gerry used every available hour along with every penny he had, to set about the substantial task of turning the house into a home, and I was invited to make a conducted tour as he was about to finish decorating; an occasion which I found truly impressive, so the following day I telephoned Social Services to recount what I had seen.

I managed to speak to Miss Stackpole who was in charge of the case and who left me in no doubt that she was extremely busy, her curt reply giving me the impression that ours was a conversation that she did not want. I told her about Gerry's efforts in his new house but unfortunately she was quite dismissive, particularly when I suggested that she should see the house and the work which Gerry had completed.

"I'll see it in due course and it will form part of my report, but it is just unfortunate that it is a little late in the day and I suspect has been done for the purposes of the case."

"Well of course it's for the purposes of the case. That's the whole idea isn't it? He was given that time to show what he could do and what steps he could take in relation to providing a home for the child."

"I'll be the judge of that," said Miss Stackpole with studied disinterest.

"Yes, but I thought it might just help."

"Again, I've just told you, I will be the judge of that and I will take into account such matters as I think are appropriate."

I got the distinct impression that Miss Stackpole was not impressed with me or my client, and I was conscious that we were heading towards a row, so with discretion this time seeming to be the better part of valour, I decided she was antagonistic enough without my making matters worse, so left it at that. One of the things I have learned about court cases is that it's not always what you say, but what you leave out that can be important, so I concluded my conversation by simply saying that I was trying to act in my client's best interests, to which Miss Stackpole grunted her condescending acknowledgement and the conversation was over.

I was angry and in a way I was annoyed with myself for not having taken her to task, but what would that have achieved? One of the difficulties we encounter in my profession is that sometimes when you are in the right you cannot say so for fear of offending someone who holds sanction over your case; which is why so many lawyers are called two-faced ...... sometimes they have to be.

My brooding was interrupted by Vera George, our new cleaner.

"Want a cup of tea duck?"

"Yes please Mrs George, two sugars."

"You shouldn't be having sugar, you should have Canderel, it's much better for you. Too much sugar can lead to wind."

I hurriedly put the piece of chocolate I was eating into my drawer.

"It always gets me like that if I have a lot of sweet stuff. I get terrible wind," said Mrs George, "Terrible, and let me tell you, that is real pain."

The thought of Mrs George walking like John Wayne because of her physical difficulties made me shudder and I had certainly not realised just how many people suffered from that affliction.

"Anyway, I've brought you a piece of carrot cake which I baked yesterday."

"Oh, lovely," I said, not wanting to cause offence even though I don't like carrot cake, but she was watching so I felt under an obligation to eat it. It was tasteless apart from a slight hint of carrot, and it simply confirmed that this was the vegetable I hated most. As I chewed through the substance I smiled, nodded approvingly and Mrs George smiled back, but again she waited whilst I ate another piece, finally giving me a third to save until later.

"Wonderful," I said, "I'll have that later," and I put it on the side of my desk.

"I'll bring you some rhubarb crumble tomorrow, that's what I'm making tonight."

I nodded and smiled again in the certain knowledge that that was the fruit I hated most!

The telephone rang and Tracey told me that Brenda Bluett was in reception for her appointment.

Big Brenda Bluett was a woman who feared no one. Her strong muscular arms led to hands which were about the size of a garden spade. She was very manly and her forte in life was arm-wrestling, but there wasn't a woman in Rotherham to beat her so she concentrated on the men.

Every time I met her in town she had her Rottweiler/Alsatian cross 'Tiger' with her. It was the most easy-going beast I'd ever seen so it was a great surprise to me to see Brenda waiting in my reception clutching what looked like a Rotherham Magistrates Court summons.

"It wasn't his fault," she blurted out. "Don't let 'em take 'im off me!"

"It's all right Brenda, calm down. What is the problem?"

"The coppers 'ave given me this," she said handing me the court summons.

I read the narrative as quickly as I could.

"This is a summons under the Dogs Act, Brenda," I said. "It would appear that the police are applying to the court for an Order that you should keep Tiger under control."

"What does that mean?" asked Brenda.

"Well it seems as though he's been involved in something which has placed a member of the public at risk."

"It was that bloody postman," she said. "Tiger hates postmen. Whenever he sees one he goes barmy, I've told you this before."

"Yes, I remember you telling me some weeks ago. Is that what's happened here?"

"Yes. The postman came down the drive and Tiger was out. He just went for him. Whenever he sees that uniform he goes barmy."

I looked at the summons and the accompanying papers and it seemed that Tiger had indeed fallen out with a postman and had bitten him on the left buttock. The police had the power to bring a summons to either apply to the court for an animal to be destroyed or at least an Order that it should be kept under control. It's rather like a suspended sentence for the dog in that if he does it again the police have the right to issue proceedings requesting its destruction.

"Well don't worry too much Brenda because they're not asking for an Order that Tiger be destroyed, just that you keep him under proper control."

I explained the ramifications of such an Order which seemed to appease Brenda somewhat.

"Supposing the Magistrates think he should be topped?"

"I don't think they will Brenda but next time I think it would be a certainty."

"Will you go to court with me?"

"Of course I will," I replied reluctantly, knowing that Legal Aid wasn't available for this sort of case.

"Will Tiger 'ave to go?"

"No," I replied, "He won't have to be at court as I don't think he would actually understand what they were saying to him anyway."

Brenda forced a courteous laugh.

"No, I don't suppose he would."

"The other problem is that if there's a postman on the Bench, he might 'ave a go at him."

"Well, he won't be in his uniform will he if he is," said Brenda.

"No, I suppose not," I replied smiling, giving away my joke, "But leave it to me and we'll look after you."

Brenda went away reasonably happy and just then the door sprang open and in walked the Honourable Sean Page.

"Good morning old bean. I was just passing so I thought I'd say hello and see if you had any whisky I could borrow."

He sat down in my leather armchair and I poured him a glass of our favourite, Canadian Club as he related a story which invited me to attend a fancy dress ball with him.

"Not a chance. I hate that sort of thing but thanks for asking. Who are you going as? Adolf Hitler?"

"No, something far more unusual."

"Benito Mussolini?"

"No, better than him."

"The Pope?"

"No."

"Well, you've got me. I've no idea," I said impatiently.

"Louis Armstrong!"

"Louis Armstrong?"

"Yes, the great guitarist."

"But Louis Armstrong played the trumpet."

"No he didn't."

"Yes he did, he had a gravel voice."

"Yes, that's him. I'll go dressed up and carrying a guitar."

I saw no point in argument and I declined the offer to go as Batman or Robin, which disappointed Pagey somewhat, but we later compromised with Pagey going as Louis Armstrong and me not going at all.

The following week Pagey went to the fancy dress ball and I sweated over Gerry Woodward's court papers.

The Social Services had prepared a written statement for the court, which came down very heavily in favour of a Care Order. Miss Stackpole had made her decision without taking into account Gerry's recent efforts, which she dismissed as being carried out just to impress the court without any real possibility of being sustained.

The hearing took place in court three at the Moorgate Courthouse where I represented Gerry Woodward whilst Social Services were represented by a council solicitor supported by Miss Stackpole and her assistant, together with three other members of staff. They must have cleaned out their entire offices of personnel just for one case! Our supporter's bench of just Gerry and me looked painfully inadequate but then we couldn't compete with the reserves of finance at the Council's disposal.

We had a fair bench and Miss Stackpole opened the case; surely the most 'anti-defendant' case I had ever heard, in which her scathing attacks upon Gerry and his circumstances were so one-sided that I almost lost my temper. Throughout the morning Miss Stackpole threw every bag of manure in the armoury and left me thinking that there was a vendetta against Gerry and us.

Gerry on the other hand gave as good as he got in the witness box, much to Miss Stackpole's annoyance and he even admitted the problems he had had with drink, but even more astonishing, he accepted he hadn't fully recovered. He came over as a man more worthy of sympathy than anything else but his honesty was to count against him, because despite our attempts to show what improvements had been made in his lifestyle, the court were suspicious and even commented that by Gerry's own admission he was still having problems with drink. In an endeavour to dispel their fears I pointed out that his honesty with the court was worthy of great credit and showed a man who was not willing to fudge his responsibilities.

I thought I had done enough to avoid the care order and let Scott go home, even if he had to be subject to a supervision order, which would still mean a lot of involvement with Social Services, but the Magistrates thought differently.

Scott was taken away from Gerry as the Magistrates made a care order, and I found it hard to accept the decision because I had allowed sentiment to creep into my consideration. I'll never forget the sight of Scott being led away from the court, almost like a criminal but without a conviction.

We would be able to bring our own proceedings after three months had expired if we were able to show that circumstances had changed which would allow the court to consider the case again. I decided that we would try again, provided that Gerry could stay away from the bottle and in fairness to him, he was determined too.

Miss Stackpole was delighted and preened herself as she wallowed in her empty victory.

She had won the battle but she wasn't going to win the war if I had anything to do with it.

Chapter Ten

I Try Cruising and
Meet an Undertaker

It was September 1986 and I had never worked harder in my life, or at least that is what I thought then, but I was enjoying my work and such trappings of success which it brought.

We were becoming well-known in the locality which meant we attracted a fair amount of work but an abundance of raffle tickets from a number of contacts who thought that we were fair game for sales.

One such raffle was quite expensive, with tickets at ten pounds each but the star prize was a car and the second prize a cruise on the famous P & O shipping line, travelling to such places of exotica as Greece, Egypt and Israel.

I had quite forgotten about my ticket including the fact that the grand draw was to take place at a Gala Dinner at a large hotel in Sheffield and I hadn't been invited to the gathering where in any event the tickets were £50 each.

I was sitting in my office preparing to go to court when Wilf brought in my post, amongst which, there were the usual bills and demands for cigarettes or Red Cross parcels from Armley jail but one letter in particular caught my eye. It was from the charitable organisation that had responsibility for the raffle and I could not believe its contents. According to them I had won second prize in the grand raffle, namely an eight night cruise for two, which would include visits to Piraeus in Greece, which would also take us to the Acropolis, Haifa in Israel for a trip to Bethlehem and Jerusalem but best of all Alexandria in Egypt to see the Sphinx and pyramids at Giza, the Cairo Museum and the fabulous Tutankhamun mask.

We boarded the ship in the famous Piraeus Harbour and after finding our way to our cabin we joined most of the travellers on the deck to wave to scores of uninterested Greeks as the ship left the harbour to the strains of 'We are Sailing' from a slightly out of tune Piraeus School band. The playing was not of the best standard and I couldn't help singing the words, 'We are drowning' to the familiar melody.

As I was standing by the gangway enjoying the band, I became aware of a bald gentleman with a young face standing next to me and we struck up a conversation. Most people are in good spirits at the start of a cruise but also most of them are full of spirit during the remainder of the voyage and this trip was to be no exception.

We discussed the various ports of call and agreed to share a drink if we should bump into each other later that evening, then after completing a tour of the ship we returned to our cabin to be re-united with our luggage before setting off on an eagerly awaited tour to the Acropolis and the beautiful Parthenon.

We were provided with some written material as we set off on our journey to meet the legends of ancient Greece somewhat unprepared for the yellow mass of pollution which hung above this historic city and we were told by the guide of the great problems this had caused. But then the Parthenon came into view from within our pleasantly air-conditioned coach: a most incredible sight and I spent a fabulous day in considerable awe walking amongst the ruins, hanging onto every word of the local guide, who told me afterwards that he had worked there for fifteen years on a five day week, forty-eight weeks a year basis doing four tours per day.

I ventured the question, "Do you think you will get to like it?" but my humour was lost on the guide who left me and set about yet another visit attempting to create the same enthusiasm with which he greeted me.

He set off into the distance extolling the virtues of the architecture to a Japanese group who could not speak English and whilst I am not a linguist it was fairly evident that he couldn't speak Japanese, but he spent the majority of that tour posing for photographs. I could imagine the Japanese photograph album with his picture in prime position bearing the caption, 'This was the guide who could not speak Japanese'.

All the events of the day are mapped out in a day sheet which gives you the various options for participation if you should be so interested, and someone suggested that it was rather like Butlins. However nothing could be further from the truth and with all respect to Butlins, cruising is vastly different.

My favourite part of the on-board activities were the meals, which were always a grand affair, particularly the seven-course dinners, and we shared a table with David and Linda Selley, two rich people from Chesterfield who were really good company. They both worked in the family textile import/export business, were quick to enjoy a really good laugh and consequently we got on well. Our own table was situated directly opposite a large circular one seating ten people of whom we shall hear more shortly and formal nights were on alternate evenings when the dress code was dinner jacket and black tie. Pre-dinner drinks were served in a variety of bars where the ladies could use the event to show off their latest designer-wear in an attempt to keep up with the Jones's.

The first formal evening was quite an occasion as people nibbled nervously at a variety of aperitifs, scrutinising each arrival to the cocktail bar and then scandalously discussing the likely value of the newcomer's dress, whilst smiling sweetly in false approval.

On one such night we arrived at the doors to the grand dining-room just as the dinner gong was sounded and we trooped into the dining-hall to be welcomed by an array of smartly-dressed waiters offering carefully contoured plastic smiles with an eye on the tips at the end of the cruise.

The service was superb, which more than lived up to the quality of the food and there was an extensive wine cellar which could only have been appreciated by the true connoisseur so I resisted the temptation to break fresh ground and concentrated on the traditional house red.

Before the meal started my attention was drawn to the large circular table nearby and it was interesting to study the characters who were seated there.   There was a tall, rather distinguished man of late years who looked like a retired army colonel sitting with his wife, who was also tall, similarly distinguished with a snipe nose and a rather arrogant air.   She appeared to be less than happy at sharing a dining-table with the lower echelons who were in fact represented by another couple of similar years.   These people I assessed to have been involved in middle management, being of a pleasant disposition, courteous of manner and given to smiling generously at everybody. They were sitting next to a young couple, who I suspected were on honeymoon as they paid little attention to anyone except each other.

The table was then joined by an unusual figure dressed in a PVC jacket, which looked as though it had been popular with its wearer for a number of years. It was a faded brown in colour, heavily marked with grease stains and further distinguished by a number of severe creases. He wore trousers fashioned from some form of rustic weave with a partially open fly and a pair of suede chukka boots, which gave him something of the appearance of the circus comic. His hair was unkempt and stuck out at the side of his head as though it had been sprayed with clear liquid concrete, surmounting a face which was bright red and bloated, caused by either an excess of sun or alcohol, or both. His only other distinguishing feature was that he was extremely drunk.

He sat between the colonel and his wife and the couple from middle management, with the ladies on each side. He broke wind as he sat down and laughed raucously, elbowing the colonel's wife, grinning lasciviously.

The wine waiter arrived and the man whom we shall henceforth refer to as the 'PVC Man' ordered a litre of house red and a pint of lager, in response to which the colonel's wife looked down her nose at him then gently moved the hem of her beautiful yellow dress over her knee and out of harm's way.

Now the amusing thing about drunks is that they are extremely bad at attempting to conceal the fact that they are drunk, so when he made an attempt to introduce himself and to enable him to shake hands with the young man opposite he had to stand up to lean slightly over the table, which caused him to break wind again. The

161

colonel's wife was appalled and began to state her considerable disquiet to her husband.

With slurred speech he ordered his meal and when the colonel's wine arrived, PVC Man took hold of the bottle, filled his glass to the brim and drank it without taking a breath.   He giggled like a schoolboy, nudging the colonel's wife with his elbow once again, smiling and winking as if accepting homage from a guest who was spellbound with his candour and general good humour. He slurred a greeting to the other members of the table and said that his name was George.

"George PVC Man," I said to myself.   Yes, it had a certain ring about it.

By this time all the tables around us had focused their attention upon this rather sad but colourful character and the more he attempted to engage in conversation, the more stupid he looked and the more pathetic he sounded.

He then sat back in his chair as if resting until his soup arrived and we watched expectantly as his head began to move forward until, inch by inch, his chin was on his chest. It was a safe bet then that his upper frame would begin to slump forward and everyone was intrigued to see what would then happen to him.   They were not long in suspense as his face hit the bowl of soup at a perfect angle causing him to rear up quickly, so spraying leek and potato soup all around him.

The colonel's wife was especially annoyed and with comments such as "Oh really," and "My God Angus," gave voice to her displeasure.

"Nice soup that," said PVC Man laughing as he attempted to wipe his face with the tablecloth.

He then squeezed the left knee of the colonel's wife, and winked, grinning offensively.

"You horrible little man," said the colonel's wife, as she stood up to march over to the restaurant manageress. As she walked past us I noticed a soup-stained handprint halfway up the beautiful yellow dress, where PVC Man had squeezed her leg.

"Let's have another drink," said PVC Man, who then leaned across the table to seize the young couple's bottle of wine. Before the young man could protest, PVC Man brought the bottle back to his side of the table and again broke wind before sitting down. He poured out a glassful and quaffed it as though his life depended upon it, before setting about drinking his lager, which spilled down his chin and onto his shirt. By this time the lady from middle management had had enough, so she too left the table.

Try as we might we others were unable to completely stifle our laughter; I myself was doubled up with something akin to real pain, and in no condition to even attempt to eat my meal. Other tables nearby had by now started to focus their attention upon Mr PVC man and the restaurant manageress, a very attractive and amiable lady, decided that diplomacy would be the order of the day so spoke to Mr PVC Man very respectfully but firmly, suggesting that he had had enough. It was almost as if there was a race to consume the entire litre of wine he had purchased, before he was induced to leave the table but Jan, the manageress, was emphatic that he should leave, much to the disappointment of the tables nearby.

PVC Man uttered his protestations in what appeared to me to be a completely foreign language, which made it even more bizarre until the deputy restaurant manager arrived to take PVC Man by the arm, assisted by Jan who took the other arm. He was thus escorted from the chair, but not before he had slumped forward slightly with his head landing over the bust of the lady from middle management, providing him with a considerable view of her cleavage.

He was swiftly pulled upright by the manager as Mr PVC Man signed off by pointing to the lady's cleavage and giving the thumbs-up sign in approval.

The colonel's wife re-appeared to unreservedly state her disgust and could hardly be blamed for failing to see the funny side of it in view of the still visible handprint on her dress which was capable of ready misinterpretation by the uninformed.

The following day I decided to attend one of the afternoon lectures given by a local guide who had been brought in to explain the organised trip to Bethlehem and Jerusalem. Aided by a substantial selection of slides and video films he was able to give us a potted version of the history of the area and also a list of do's and don'ts.

I made my way to the top deck open air restaurant to meet up with one of the most extensive wine lists I think I had seen in a long time and as I waited to place my order I became aware of a familiar face perusing the wine list. It was my bald acquaintance bedecked in multicoloured T-shirt, shorts and the traditional British issue sandals and I was drawn to a smudge of suntan cream on his already reddening pate. He was of average height with a large build and generous waistline, seemingly at odds with his Bermuda shorts which had found their mark well below his abdomen, thus allowing the thirty-eight inch waist shorts to be worn below his forty-one inch waist. For all the world, this was an Englishman abroad and he didn't need a Union

Jack about his person to make it apparent where he was from.

As I was reflecting upon this, a steward walked past me carrying a very large sheet of Perspex mirror where I observed myself bedecked in striped Bermuda shorts and multicoloured T-shirt. Another Englishman abroad I thought to myself and smiled at the similarity. The comparison of our midriffs led me to the thought that we could be related.

We exchanged a nod as we were being served with our T-bone steak whereupon my English acquaintance looked across to me and in an attempt to begin a conversation said, "You like steak then?"

Quick as a flash or so I thought I replied.

"No, I'm a vegetarian, this is for the dog."

We both laughed and walked back to share a table, where after introductions, our respective families sat down together to enjoy a rather sumptuous meal, achieving an instant rapport in the process.

During the meal we extended our introductions: his name was Malcolm Garton who lived in Hull with his lovely wife Barbara and his daughter Andrea. During the conversation we agreed to guess each other's profession and my first guess was that he was a chef but then I decided upon some form of business representative or sales person.

We enjoyed some good banter over luncheon and when we got to the sweet course it became fairly obvious why my friend had such a large waistline for he tucked into the baked alaska with considerable relish. I continued the guessing game, suggesting a travelling salesman or a prison officer, and when I told him that I was a solicitor he didn't believe me because, as he put it, "Solicitors are generally reserved, cultured, smart and have a considerable presence."

"You bald-headed bastard," I thought to myself.

I gave up guessing his job and he put me out of my misery by telling me that he was an undertaker.

I was getting over the initial shock when the deck entertainment started in the form of Errol Wiseman and his Caribbean Calypso Band. I later spoke to the lead of the band, a very pleasant chap with extremely dark skin and brilliant white teeth, who told me that the furthest that he had ever travelled in the world was on this cruise. His normal job was as a porter in Watford Market!

As I listened to the music I gazed at the harbour setting where looking east there was the Greek mainland stretching into the distance, contrasted against a brilliant blue sky but to the west you were greeted by docks which disclosed from end to end the wreckage of sunken ships, whose rotting hulls added a touch of the macabre to the view.

The 'smart money' was therefore on the eastern perspective with the sound of the steel band ringing in your ears and the warm evening sun causing eerie silhouettes over the other ships anchored off the harbour.

It wasn't long before Malcolm and I were recounting a variety of stories and anecdotes based upon our respective professions.

We had a wonderful day and agreed that we would dine together that night, arranging to meet in one of the lounges, but I was early so I decided to take a stroll around the deck where I watched from the stern of the ship as the sun was setting on the horizon. It was a magnificent sight seated at

166

a table facing this wonderful view and gazing at the ocean where the sun's reflection danced from wave to wave as the ship ploughed relentlessly through the calm sea and the steel band played on with commendable empathy. The atmosphere on board was equally incredible, being luxuriously embellished by people walking the decks with their pre-dinner cocktails, resplendent in their elegant sequinned dresses ...... And the women!

I walked to the rail at the end of the stern of the ship and as I looked out to sea I felt good, warm and contented.

"James Bond would do this," I thought to myself. "White tux, carnation and............."

My thoughts were interrupted by a friendly waiter who offered to fetch me a drink,

"Vodka Martini please," I said playing out the role for my own amusement, "Shaken not stirred."

I returned to my thoughts and began to dream almost like Billy Liar, only to be disturbed again by the arrival of the waiter with my drink whereat I signed the cheque with a flourish, the hint of a smile and took a large mouthful only to find that the drink was rather stronger than I imagined, making me cough at the first swallow. As my eyes watered I returned to my thoughts only to realise that the tune the steel band were playing was a reggae version of *'Tie Me Kangaroo Down Sport'*.

The time had come to meet up with my new friends and as I got up a bald, fat and rather squat American wearing a white tux took my place at the rail.

"Makes you feel like James Bond," he drawled in his Texan accent.

"Yes, I suppose it does," I replied in an attempt to be agreeable, but my words were drowned by the sound of the ship's horn that blared out at the opportune moment.

"Yes sir, it sure does.   I agree with you yee hah", he shouted as if ready to mount a horse.

"Bloody Yank", I thought as I walked off in search of the sunset.

Everytime I saw that bugger thereafter he referred to me as Mr Bond and I referred to him as Davy Crockett, which he took as a great compliment.

"Hey yee hah Mr Bond, have a nice day," he would say.

"Yee hah Davy," I would reply, "Go and milk a buffalo".

"Hey, what a sense of humour these Yorkshire guys have got," he joked, addressing no one except himself.

When the bell rang for dinner our group walked down to the dining room and as we entered we were all introduced to the Captain.   My American friend was in front of us and on meeting the Captain he couldn't help but try to be what he thought was amusing.

"Hey, if you're the Captain and you're here in the dining room, who is driving the boat, yee hah?"   He laughed, enjoying his own joke.

The Captain was about to explain but the Yank disappeared into the dining room, slapping the backs of the other guests as he went, and it mattered not whether they were men or women, they all got a slap just the same.

As I was introduced, the Captain was observing Davy Crockett who was leaving many a coughing subject in his wake.   Before the Captain could speak I looked towards the American gentleman and said,

"I think the expression is 'go and milk a buffalo'."

"Quite so," said the Captain trying to retain formality.

I went into the dining room and seeing the Yank I slapped him on the back, crying "Yee hah Davy," as I did so.

The Captain merely smiled and winked. I think he understood and appreciated my irony.

We enjoyed a marvellous meal, with the sweet forming the grand finale, when the lights were dimmed and after a drum roll the waiters marched in with the baked alaska.

The Yank was sitting near our table and I noted his comment on sight of the flaming dish.

"Hey Martha, my pudding is on fire!" shouted Davy Crockett. I was not sure whether he was joking or not.

We retired to the lounge for coffee and liqueurs and thereafter the Cabaret. At midnight I lost £5 on the roulette wheel which was enough for me, because I reckoned my money was too hard earned to gamble it away on the drop of a pea!

The 'gambling room' was situated in the piano bar at the stern of the ship, where the pianist was playing suitable background music for the fly-boys of the cruise to show off with their Armani suits, Rolex watches and large wads of £20 notes. I walked into the gathering with my Marks and Spencer dinner suit, Seiko watch and 3 crisp new fivers......but I was prepared to blow all three. I bought some chips (£5 worth) and stood at the table as though I knew what I was doing – a 'devil may care' entrepreneur with £5 worth of chips, a glass of milk stout and my bow tie hanging harmlessly down by the front of my collar in its original pre-tied state. I thought I looked the part but, on reflection, 'fart' might have been a better term.

I couldn't play for two reasons:

1.   I couldn't get a place; and

2.   I didn't know how.   Nonetheless, I tried to look as though I did and stood casually in the queue.

A man with dark swarthy features leaned towards me conspiratorially as if about to impart a great secret.

"Do you think you'll win then?" I asked naively.

"Probably," said Omar Sharif.

"You see you need to remember three things.

1.   Feel the game.

2.   See the pee.

3.   Watch the Croupier.

Got it?" he said mysteriously.

"Yes," I said, "Got it," as though I understood every word, when really I hadn't got a clue.

Within minutes Omar had made his mark, £20 on Number 26.

"No more bets Mesdames and Messieurs," said 'Henri' with a false French accent.   His real name was Henry Parsons and he was from Mablethorpe.

"Number 26!"

I couldn't believe it.   Surely just luck.   I watched even closer as he put £50 on number 36.

"No more bets Mesdames and Messieurs."

Omar winked at me as number 36 came up.

"I'm tired," said Omar, "I go to my bed," and off he went with about £3,000 of P & O's money.

His place was left empty and I found myself a somewhat reluctant occupant of his seat.   I tried to look as casual as possible, giving a knowing nod and 'nonchalant' smile to the other players as they waited eagerly for the next game.

Hands moved across the table with considerable speed but all I could think of was Omar's instructions, when an elderly German woman joined me in the next seat and in a soft spoken voice sought my advice.

"Good evening, how are you?"

"Very well thank you," I replied.

"I have never played before, have you any advice?"

"Certainly," I said, laying claim to expertise which I hadn't got.

"There are three things to remember.

1.   See the game.

2.   Have a pee.

3.   Feel the Croupier,"

I said with astonishing aplomb, believing I had reiterated Omar's principles faithfully.   The German woman looked at me rather perplexed and I proceeded to put £5 on Number 13.

"No more bets Mesdames and Messieurs, no more bets please."

"Number 4."

"Oh bollocks," I announced.

"I beg your pardon," said the German woman.

"Oh er I lost, slight miscalculation," I said as I tried to laugh off the cost of the equivalent of six pints of duty free lager.

I did not play the next game but watched as my German friend won on number 13.

"Oh bollocks," I said under my breath, "Bloody Kraut," and walked off to the piano bar.

"Do you know any German songs?" I said to the pianist.

"What about Lili Marlene?" came the reply from a bored and slightly drunk pianist.

"That'll do," I said as I drank my Crème de Menthe frappée.

I tried one more go on the roulette and watched how the most skilful newcomer to roulette became the richest German on board.

I lost another six pints, ate a giant gammon sandwich and decided that roulette wasn't for me.

My family and I spent the remainder of the week with the Gartons forming a friendship which continues to this very day. I will long remember Malcolm's enthusiasm to enter every competition during the ship's itinerary and to this day, I am told, there is a mark on the funnel where he failed miserably in the twelve bore shooting competition.

It was Malcom's birthday later that week and it is tradition on P & O Cruises that when there is a birthday waiters will stand round your table and sing 'Happy Birthday' in a mixture of accents and keys to honour the person concerned. The Head Waiter stood on my left and asked me for the birthday boy's name so it could be included in the song.

"Baldy," I informed him for a joke, pointing to his head.

"OK," said the waiter, not seeing the funny side, and before I could stop them six waiters began to sing,

"Happy Birthday, dear Baldy, Happy Birthday to you."

They couldn't see the joke, and neither could Malcolm, but about 80 other guests in the dining room thought it was a hoot.

The waiters were of mixed origin including one chap from Goa who had great difficulty with English, so frequently got his words mixed up, and there was one incident where Malcolm wanted to keep the cork from the bottle of Champagne as a memento. He asked Mahatma for the cork but was promptly presented with a bottle of Coke, so Malcolm pointed out that he actually wanted the cork, and

172

it was with profuse apology and some embarrassment that Mahatma again left, to return beaming with a coat.   I seized it quickly so as not to upset the waiter and thanked him generously for his assistance.   Malcolm took his Coca Cola and caftan and off he went.

Overnight we sailed to Alexandria in Egypt and consistent with P & O's military precision the coaches were waiting at the quayside for the long journey into Cairo.

Our ship had docked in the remarkable city of Alexandria, which affords the effect of stepping back in time, because I would imagine that parts of it have not changed since the 1940's, so providing the visitor with a sharp contrast between the modern high rise hotels and the seedy back streets.   After 3 hours travelling we arrived at the city of Cairo, following a most fascinating and rewarding journey where I found myself intoxicated by the sights and sounds of the city.   The streets were filthy, the roads appalling and the traffic an absolute joke but there was an excitement about the place that I have not felt anywhere else in the world.

I remember one incident in particular; as we drove into the city travelling along one of the market places I noticed a shop which had several large black objects hanging outside on display.   I asked the Guide what they were and watched the shop owner emerge, colliding as he did so with one of the hanging objects, when to my amazement, this caused it to become white, a change which seemed to take place in an instant.

When I looked again, the object became grey and then black again, which made me realise that the black objects were in fact swarms of flies.   Apparently they were cheeses much favoured by the indigenous population and equally appreciated by the local squadrons of flies as well.

When we arrived in the centre of Cairo we were shown into the Hilton Hotel for lunch, where we were given all the usual warnings; don't drink the water; don't eat the salad; peel the fruit; don't have any ice cubes in your drinks etc, but we had a grand lunch nevertheless before setting off for the famous Cairo Museum and Tutankhamun's Mask.

The Museum was as busy as the City itself but it was an old building and lacked the necessary air conditioning, and although not as stylish as its Louvre counterpart in Paris it had a special atmosphere unlike anywhere I had visited before.

We visited a number of rooms displaying artefacts from various Egyptian dynasties, giving us an insight into the opulence of the period, but there was little opportunity to gaze in detail as we were carried along in the torrent of visitors towards a room in the distance.

After half an hour we approached a room, busier than the rest, and when I walked through the door my eyes were immediately attracted to the main exhibit - Tutankhamun's Mask. I marvelled at its perfection. It was probably one of the most beautiful objects I have ever seen and I was transfixed by this exquisite sight, so much so that I didn't notice the armed guards standing by each corner of the display case. A rather knowledgeable visitor informed me that it was impossible to place a value on the collection, and I was not surprised.

Unfortunately, I was moved on by the ever-present inspectors who were hurrying the visitors along to avoid congestion and I regret that our tight schedule did not permit us to spend more time savouring the spectacle of Egypt's triumphant past. Our next visit was to the Pyramids and the unforgettable face of the Sphinx.

The weather was good, it was warm and dry and the air-conditioned coach helped to make it a pleasant journey with plenty of interest along the way. In many ways I was appalled by some of the sights as street vendors sold fruit and cooked food in the gutter itself on make-shift stoves. Domestic animals were allowed to wander amongst the stalls but despite all this there was an ambience which I couldn't describe, and then I witnessed my first sighting of the Pyramids.

I find it difficult to describe how I felt, seeing this great sight which had fascinated millions of people before me.

The atmosphere was incredibly vibrant, with musicians and all manner of street artists, jugglers and the like performing their acts. I was intrigued by one of the horsemen showing off his skills to the accompaniment of the street musicians, whilst maintaining his seat astride a beautiful white Arabian horse which was highly trained in the art of dancing on its back legs as it performed to an awe inspired and appreciative audience. The peddlers were an absolute nuisance, positioning themselves in front of you, at the side of you, behind you and in your pockets. They were the most persistent and disagreeable people I had ever met.

I was advised by one of the attendants from the coach to shout to the peddlers the words 'Shim Shee'. I asked him what it meant and he said he didn't know but it always caused great offence, which is not surprising since I later found out that 'Shim Shee' was Egyptian for something akin to 'sod off you odious little turd'.

I actually saw one group of peddlers literally lift a man onto a donkey to take him on a ride around the grand Pyramid, and it stood out a mile that he did not want to go but they would not be deterred, despite his cries for help.

The other trick they perform is to talk you into having a ride on a camel and then refuse to let you off until you pay them more than the agreed price. It was said that you could always tell a Scotsman in the party because they were riding on the camels all day.

At the end of our visit I had time to sit and gaze at one of the most beautiful sights I have ever seen, as the sun moved towards the horizon, highlighting the Sphinx and the Pyramids in its wake.

My pal Malcolm became the subject of the sales force's efforts because having a bald head they thought he would benefit from wearing a Lawrence of Arabia type head-dress. Their sales technique was incredible and when Malcolm explained that he preferred to leave his bald patch open to the elements for the purpose of a suntan (he was lying of course), the peddlers suggested that he could cut away the top of the head-dress so that the patch would be exposed to the sun.

One peddler must have sold Tutankhamun's original necklace no less than thirty times that day so perhaps Tutankhamun had a number of spares? I recall one peddler attempting to sell me an item he described as a 'Jambar', or something similar. It looked to me like a camel turd and, having no need of such an item, I told him to "Shim Shee off," only to be told that it was very tasty. Our guide said that it was a form of chocolate cake, but I got the impression that a camel had to eat and digest it first before you could buy it.

I saw two Americans hand over their camera to a peddler who offered to take a photograph for them, but who also kept telling them to move back until he was far enough away to escape with their camera!

We returned to Cairo from where we continued on the long drive to the Harbour in Alexandria, and I could not help thinking what tales those cobbled streets could tell; murder; intrigue; kidnap; and the country's innate ability to sell camel turds.

When we arrived back at the ship, I was ready for a nice bath and a large gin and tonic before dinner but as we boarded my attention was drawn to 'Malcolm of Arabia' who was wearing the Arabian hat with a hole cut in the top to let the sun shine through.

That night we set sail for Haifa in Israel and my run-in with the schizophrenics in customs.

Israel is a place I have always wanted to visit, without really wishing to test the warmth and content of its hospitality with an overnight stay, so a cruise was the ideal way to do it, except that I found the Israeli customs officials rude and ignorant and possessed nothing to commend them.

We were to be taken to various points of interest on a whistle stop jaunt, before returning to the ship and departing fairly quickly for our next destination. I appreciate that such tours only scratch the surface, but this was sufficient for my purposes and I put my name down for the trips to Jerusalem and Bethlehem, since these places were of great interest to me. In many ways I was to be disappointed.

Malcolm had also booked himself onto this trip and we told the organisers that we wished to travel together, because my daughter was ill with a chest infection at the time, necessitating my wife remaining on the ship but insisting that I set off with my cameras into Jerusalem.

It was a very long drive from Haifa, but time seemed unimportant as we took in the many interesting things to see en-route, including a number of communes with their extremely well ordered and organised vineyards and orange groves.

Unfortunately our first port of call was Bethlehem and quite frankly I was disappointed. It was much like Blackpool, with neon lights and advertisements, though thankfully free of the pestering beggars that we had been used to in Egypt. Nevertheless, in my view it was geared towards the 'Big Sell' because everywhere you went, somebody wanted to sell you something, and I was particularly appalled to find that even at the most religious sites everyone, including the priests, were actively trying to sell 'holy' candles and 'holy' water from the River Jordan. I found it distasteful, particularly when, having bought a 'holy' candle, you had to buy a 'holy' match with which to light it. 'Holy' lighters were extra, although they did have the place of purchase endorsed thereon. When I went into the Church I lit my candle and together with the other hundred and fifty or so people who were present, gasped in horror as it became promptly extinguished. Quick as a flash someone tried to sell me a crucifix and, feeling so incredibly uncomfortable I bought one, only to be disappointed later when I found that the item had been made in Taiwan.

We followed the route alleged to have been taken by Christ on his journey to the cross, which I found to be most interesting, although I was confused as to which parts of the city were owned by whom.

From there we moved on to the infamous Garden of Gethsemane, where there are lime trees which have been carbon dated to prove that they are over 2,000 years old, so would certainly have been there at the time of Christ. The place was unusually tranquil, but the Wailing Wall beckoned and Prayers were in progress when we arrived. I stopped for a few moments to watch the population in worship but in many ways it was hard to imagine that such religious fervour could invoke such anger and hostility.

After the crowd had dispersed we were allowed to view the area and I don't know what it is about such important monuments, but I always anticipate that they are much larger than they really are. This view was apparently shared by one interested party behind me who summed it up in a rather unflattering way via the comment, "Well, it's a wall."

The remainder of the day was spent in the various churches in the area, in particular the Holy Sepulchre, where I bought another bottle of 'Holy' water and a couple of candles. I found the place fascinating but again I was rather disappointed with the commercial emphasis which seems to dominate these occasions.

When we returned to Customs I got the distinct impression that the people were pleased to have taken our money, but delighted we were leaving. Nevertheless, it was a visit that I would not have missed and one day I would like to go back to stay for a while to see if I can understand the place and its people, since I don't feel that because of the short time I was there I have been able to express a completely constructive and balanced view. However the impressions I have so far recorded are what struck me at the time.

We were to sail that night to the Port of Izmir in Turkey which was to signal the end of our trip, and I returned to the ship with my camera bag full of pictures and movie film chronicling our journey. Taking my daily walk around the ship I managed to secure an outside table at the stern rail near the pool as the ship weighed anchor and steamed out of the harbour. It was 76 degrees, the fresh sea breeze was incredibly welcome and Davy Crockett was nowhere to be seen.

"Vodka Martini?" asked the waiter.

"Have you got a pint of lager?" I asked.

"Certainly sir," said the waiter.

I looked out to the disappearing coastline and for a moment my mind wandered as I watched the setting sun hide behind the horizon. "Nothing lasts forever," I thought to myself, but then the steel band began to play the James Bond theme and the waiter delivered my pint of lager, which he proudly announced had been stirred, not shaken. I realised that everyone tries to be a comic sometimes.

Chapter Eleven

Jack's Car Boot

It was a beautiful late June morning and as I walked through the car park to the office past the church I saw one of the parish volunteers busy cutting the lawns with an extremely old but still serviceable manual lawnmower. The smell of chlorophyll drifted on the warm air from the newly mown grass and the lawns themselves were the colour of emerald green, after two days of constant rain, which had brightened up the foliage on plants in the old stone containers delighting passers-by and to a lesser extent, the local cider squad who spent their day lounging around the benches in the church courtyard.

It was eight forty-five and already the winos had begun to gather, exchanging an array of bottles containing cheap sherry, cider and on giro day the odd beer or two.

The group were never troublesome in the morning but when drink had begun to take effect they could be caustic, abusive and rowdy.   They antagonised the general flow of pedestrians by their continual begging and flurries of abuse particularly when unsympathetic individuals disregarded their entreaties.   I tried not to look, but noticed one member out of the corner of my eye who was more familiar than the rest.   It was Gerry Woodward.   I ignored a request for a five pound note, only to hear the words, 'arrogant knob-head and twat-bag' ringing in my ears as I walked swiftly through the 'valley of a thousand requests' to the office door.   Discretion was everything when passing through this fragment of misguided society and I thought that a well aimed riposte, however brilliantly conceived, would have been wasted, so I pretended not to care.

When I entered the waiting room I was greeted by Ronald Arthur Mulligan, known by the peculiar nickname of Dimsey, which was based on his intellectual attainment or rather the lack of it, since suffice it to say, he was indeed truly dim. Nevertheless he had a considerable amount of charm allied to a sunny and pleasant disposition which made him almost likeable. Unfortunately he was a persistent but unsuccessful thief, and Dimsey had been charged with stealing a hundred metres of barbed wire, which had once formed a fence around a building site to protect it from thieves, but Ronnie had stolen it anyway. The building site remained intact but the fencing had gone, finding it's way into Ronnie's back yard, when unfortunately for him, so did the police. Identification of the stolen property was easy because it still had the contractors symbols fixed at intervals along the wire itself, displaying the somewhat redundant words, 'Keep Out. Trespassers will be Prosecuted'.

Ronnie greeted me with a wide grin, shaking my hand firmly in the process. He was a large chap, just over six feet tall weighing in at around sixteen stones and had the look of a nightclub bouncer about him for he was big, strong and no doubt had the ability to cause some damage should he choose to involve himself in fisticuffs. He had a very slow drawl to his speech which seemed to add a hint of comedy to his general persona.

We went into an interview room where Ronnie handed me his charge sheets, the back of which appeared to have been marinated in tomato sauce, so I unwrapped the offending paperwork rather delicately in order to safeguard my fingers from the rather disgusting looking mixture and then read the narrative of the charge.

"Are you pleading guilty to this Ronnie?" I asked.

"Well…..," said Ronnie even more slowly than usual, "The…coppers…found it in…my yard."

"Yes, so you'll be pleading guilty then?" I asked.

"Well…the police...found it…in…my…yard."

"Yes, I realise that Ronnie, but does that mean you're pleading guilty?"

"When…they…found…it…in…my…yard…they…took…it…back…to…the…police station."

"Yes I realise that so it looks like it's a guilty plea then Ronnie?"

"That's…what…I'm…trying…to…say.
I…can't…really…….well…really…I…can't………well …what…can…I…say?
In…other…words…I…really…am….."

"Stupid?" I thought to myself, conceding that although he wasn't a bad bloke, he did seem to be totally unable to say the word 'guilty'.

"Guilty!" I said in a raised voice.

"Well…yes."

"Thank God for that.   I thought you were never going to say it."

"Well…it's…like…this…….".

"No, it's all right Ronnie, don't worry, I understand entirely.   The police found it in your yard and consequently there can be absolutely no doubt that your actions entirely implied your guilt.   Is that correct?"

"Well…they…found…it…in…my…yard……"

Before he could finish I spoke the word as I wrote it down on my instructions sheet.

183

"Guilty."

To save time I directed my questions in such a way that the logical answer would have to be 'yes' or 'no', cutting down the interview from one hour to just twenty minutes. Finally I gave Ronnie the Legal Aid papers to sign and watched him carefully as he had great difficulty in signing his name. He was due at court the following Monday so I explained the procedure.

"I want you at court at 9.45am, which is a quarter to ten – in the morning of course."

"You...what?" asked Ronnie.

"Well you see the courts don't work at night, do they? I'd like you there with your best suit on and I'll see what we can do for you."

Ronnie looked perplexed.

"What's the matter Ron?" I asked.

"I...haven't...got...a...suit," said Ronnie.

"Well, can you put a collar and tie on?"

"A...collar...and...tie?" he queried.

"Yes. That means a white shirt as well, not just a collar on its own," and I laughed in the hope that he would join in with me, but he didn't. A horrible thought came instantly into my mind: that I had not explained it in enough detail, so that there were visions of him turning up with just a collar and tie but no shirt.

"An ordinary shirt and tie would do." I said.

Ronnie looked at me blankly.

"Well, anything then. Come as you are in fact if it's a problem."

"I...can't...go...like...this," said Ronnie.

To be fair he had a point, because a Mickey Mouse T-shirt with the legend 'Don't f... with Mick' and striped jogging bottoms would not necessarily gain him great favour and he had taken the point.

"If…I…turn…up…like…this…they'll…think…I'm…an …idiot."

"Get away," I replied sarcastically. "Well, just turn up in anything."

"What's anything?" he asked blankly. I left it at that.

On the day of the hearing I had a number of cases in the list including Ronnie's and I was pleased to see he had turned up bright and early, but the second thing I noticed was that he was wearing a curious suit of grey material with an almost cutaway-style jacket and on the lapel I noticed the initials RM. Ronnie caught me looking at it.

"What…do…you…think…to…this…suit?" asked Ronnie.

"I think it looks very smart Ron and it's an excellent fit, although the sleeves look a little short." In fact they only reached down to his elbows.

"That's…the…style," said Ronnie. "It's…the…new…look."

I wasn't sure about the style or the new look, but I always worked on the basis that sleeves should cover the entire arm and not just reach halfway. Otherwise the jacket was a good fit.

"It's…got…my…initials…on…it…as…well," said Ron. "It's…been…'specially made for me. Look…R M…Ronnie…Mulligan," he said pointing to the lapel.

There was little time for us to discuss his wardrobe because almost immediately the emphysemic usher called me into court, where Ronnie's case was the first on and I set about mitigating his misdemeanours to the Magistrates. The Chairperson was a lady in her sixties who was extremely courteous, her manner making her very popular amongst the defence solicitors, but she was a tough sentencer and was not impressed with Ronnie's list of previous convictions.

She told us that the Magistrates were considering a custodial sentence and consequently the case would be adjourned for the preparation of a Probation Report to look into all options of sentencing. Ronnie had missed the point entirely and when the case was adjourned for four weeks, he thought he had got off scotfree.

The procedure was that the Probation Service would contact him, would interview him about his past and then look into the reasons for his behaviour, whereupon they would make a recommendation to the court as to how he should be dealt with.

The following day I was in the rat-hole interview room speaking to a client, when one of my cases had been called on in Court Two.

As I was sitting on the solicitors' bench I looked at the defendant and couldn't help noticing that he was wearing a grey suit, cut away at the waist, with rather short sleeves, but more importantly it had the initials RM embroidered in red on the lapel. The suit was a duplicate of the one which Ronnie had worn the day before.

I looked at the court list to check the defendant's name and discovered he was called Adrian Fenton so obviously his initials were not RM. Nevertheless I was intrigued and was tempted to ask him where he had got the suit from, but I did not wish to cause offence, so as he looked a lot bigger than me I decided to leave it as it was, thinking it was just a coincidence.

The following day I was interviewing clients in my office when in walked a local ne'er-do-well called Eric Parker, whom I had known for a number of years as a bit of a character and a dab hand at removing stereos from motor vehicles by skilfully fixing their alarms so that they wouldn't go off until after he had completed the theft. He came in, sat in the interview chair, and the first thing I noticed was that he was wearing one of the grey suits with the cutaway waist and the short sleeves, which on closer scrutiny revealed the letters RM in red on the lapel.

We talked about his case, but my attention was continually drawn to his clothing and on more than one occasion I inadvertently repeated a question.

"Are tha listenin' to me or what?   That's the third time tha's asked me that?"

"I'm sorry Eric, I was a little distracted.   In fact I'll tell you what it is.   I have been wondering about your suit."

"My suit?   What's wrong with it?"

"Nothing.   It's very smart in fact, but I can't quite understand why the sleeves are so short."

"It's the new style i'nt it?   It's to save you rolling the sleeves up."

"Yes," I said, "But supposing you don't want to roll the sleeve up?"

"That's the style i'nt it, short sleeves and the cutaway waist."

The cutaway waist on Eric hadn't really worked because his extended forty-four inch waist supported a huge beer belly, which he said had cost him a fortune.

My curiosity got the better of me and I had to ask him it's origin.

"What do the initials RM mean?" I asked.

"Oh," said Eric, "That's Ricardo Monchetti."

"Who the bloody hell's Ricardo Monchetti?" I asked.

187

"That's the maker i'nt it? It's Italian. It's the new style, cutaway waist and short sleeves, and that's a Designer label."

"A Designer label?"

"Yes, a Designer label, Ricardo Monchetti. It's Italian tha knows. It's the latest import. It's going to be all the rage and this'll pull the birds."

It seemed to me that whatever Eric wore he would not be able to 'pull the birds' for he was rather fat and bald and had no teeth. The armpits of the jacket were stained with sweat and with respect to Eric he did not cut the figure of a dashing Errol Flynn.

"It's the dog's bollocks," said Eric.

"Not the dog's bollocks again!" I thought to myself. That poor dog has suffered enough.

"Where have you got the suit from Eric, if you don't mind me asking?"

"Why, does tha want one?"

"Er, not really," I said without wishing to be insulting. "I'm not too keen on the sleeves or the cutaway jacket."

"What's up with thee? It's the latest fashion this – a right bird-puller."

I couldn't help thinking on mature reflection that it did indeed look like a pair of dog's bollocks, so I persisted,

"Where did you get it from?"

"I got it from a mate of mine, he's importing them from Italy. Everybody's wearing them. You want to go out to our club tonight, all them as is available will be wearing these."

"What do you mean, available?" I asked.

"Well, it's the talk of the area this. What you do is you put one of these Ricardo Monchetti suits on and that like tells the birds that you're available."

"Available for what?"

"They see you in this latest Italian suit with the short sleeves and they come and chat you up, 'cos it's like a call sign which shouts out to 'em 'I'm 'ere if you want me. I'm available baby tha knows!'

Something somewhere told me that Eric had been had.

"Where did you get the suit from did you say?" I asked again.

"Jack Heptonstall got it for me. He's got one or two from one of his pals in Italy."

"You mean Albert's dad?" I asked.

"Yes, Albert's dad. They've all got them and they go out in them. They look great don't they?"

"Yes," I replied thoughtfully.

So Albert's dad had acquired a load of suits from goodness knows where and was flogging them all around Rotherham.

I completed my instructions and he went on his way, doubtless to the local Workingmen's Club when, I assume, all the local 'birds' without a sense of smell would drape themselves around him when the music started.

The following day I had a full list of appointments including Ronnie Mulligan, who was coming in to see me to go through his papers, together with three or four new clients whom I'd not seen before.

I was just saying farewell to a lady who'd been charged with having no television licence when I heard a commotion coming from reception. It was the sound of a dog barking and growling so I went into reception to see

189

what was happening, and there in the corner, being restrained by Big Brenda, was Tiger whilst in the other corner, trembling with fear, was Ronnie Mulligan.

"Tell 'im to sod off," said Brenda.

"Sod off Ronnie," I shouted in reply and with that Ronnie left the room and sought sanctuary in the toilet on the corridor, at which almost immediately Tiger sat down and calmly wagged his tail.

It was a most bizarre state of affairs because usually Tiger only bothered with postmen.

It was just at that moment that things began to fit, and 1 suppose if I'd been brighter I would have seen it earlier except that I wasn't actually looking for an answer at the time.   But there it was in front of me and the clues could never have been more obvious.

The jackets were cut-in at the waist.   The dog always went for   postmen.   The   initials   on   the   lapel......R M.......Ricardo Monchetti.......postmen........always goes for postmen...........R M.............the dog never goes for anyone else and indeed I had proof of it, for it bathed me in its drool on more than one occasion ...R M?... Could it be that R M was not Ricardo Monchetti but something else? That wouldn't explain the peculiar sleeves and neither would it explain the cut-away waist......but then Jack Heptonstall was the key and I was resolved to see him, if only to satisfy my own curiosity.

On the Sunday I had occasion to travel to the Worksop area to see a witness whom I had promised to see the previous week but who, owing to court commitments, had remained unvisited until now.

When I had taken the statement I required I travelled back to Rotherham but en route saw a sign for Thoresby market.

Thoresby is a very large open car boot/market where there are all manner of items to be bought and sold, so I decided to seek out some bedding plants for my garden and this was as good a place as any to call. As the weather was fine and dry I decided that a walk across the fields in pursuit of horticultural perfection was the order of the day.

I wandered around until I found a plant stall, then armed with a cardboard box full of all manner of half-hardy annuals I set off back to the car, but there on a stall in the distance I saw a large piece of cardboard with the name 'Ricardo Monchetti designer suits' written on it. My curiosity got the better of me and I walked to the stall, which was surrounded by a number of young men trying on suits with short sleeves, a cut-in waist and the letters R M printed on the lapel. There, in the middle of it, were two of Ricardo Monchetti's main British agents, Jack and Albert Heptonstall! Jack even had a tape measure hung around his neck, the personification of tailoring excellence, although what he wanted that for I had no idea.

As usual, Jack's eyes were everywhere and seeing me in the distance, he waved me over with a show of great affection.

"Now then Steve, how are you?"

"I'm well Jack, 'ow are you?"

"Oh, not too bad," said Jack, "Just trying to get a bit of 'onest work done."

I looked around the stall and noticed a large metal rack-type structure which housed a large number of suits with cutaway waists and short arms and the letter R.M. on the lapel.

There was a substantial amount of boxer shorts with no fly, a design fault which enabled him to buy them cheaply, and

191

they were advertised by a sign which read 'New look from Brazil, as worn by Eunuchs in the rain forests, for complete comfort'. Jack gave me four pairs as a present including one pair which bore the motif 'what an arse'.

Jack showed me a receipt for the shorts, which he had bought as seconds from a bankrupt stock supplier, and he was proud of all his acquisitions which showed he had the makings of a good business, selling all manner of objets d'art, with such items as an old typewriter, an exhaust for an MGB and a set of vicar's robes.

I was really interested in the jackets from Italy and so I asked Jack about them.

"The jackets are interesting Jack."

"Aye, they are, Italian designer label, Ricardo Monchetti."

"Really?"

"Aye."

"What's the real truth Jack, they aren't pinched are they?"

"Definitely not!" said Jack indignantly "I only deal in straight gear"

"To tell you the truth, I bought them for £1 each because the makers got the sleeves and waists wrong."

"I can see that."

"Aye, they're not really Italian but their stock supervisor has been there for 'is 'olidays. They were a good buy. I'm knocking them out at £50 a throw and the lads are buying all I've got"

"Ricardo Monchetti wouldn't happen to be Italian for Royal Mail would it?" I asked.

Jack looked at me with mock surprise, as did Albert who joined the end of the conversation but then almost in slow motion a smile broke out on both their faces. The smile turned into a snigger and then all three of us were engaged in raucous laughter.

It was some time before it ceased and we were joined by a customer, a thin youth with a spotty complexion and dirty hands who asked Jack about the jackets.

"Them Ricardo Monchetti jackets, 'ow much are they?

We all burst out into laughter again, which prompted the enquirer to call us a set of twats as he walked off indignantly.

The jackets were seconds, and in some cases I would have thought thirds, owing to the various design faults, but with an air of optimism and some forward thinking Jack and Albert had turned them into the designer wear of the year. Somehow I'll never be able to look at a postman in the same light again.

The following day I was parking my car near the office when I saw Big Brenda walking towards me. We met along the street and passed the time of day and Tiger covered my trousers with drool.

As I continued to walk to the office I heard Tiger barking ferociously and turned to see Brenda pulling him away from where my car was parked. Despite her considerable strength she was having a great deal of difficulty, but then I realised it was probably because I had a Ricardo Monchetti jacket on a coat hanger in the back of my car covering up the eunuch's underwear and the set of vicar's robes I had bought for Pagey!

Chapter Twelve

Failing to Like Ray Turton
And a Twitch in Time

Ray Turton was Rotherham's most unpopular bloke. He was disliked by the police, the public, the criminal fraternity, his family and most of all by me.

He has moved his affinity from one solicitor's firm to another over the years, amassing a number of convictions for deception, petty theft and offences against the Department of Health and Social Security. Wilf described him as one of the unfortunate products of the welfare state. I described him as an evil grabbing bastard, totally devoid of any morals or sense of responsibility whatsoever.

Wilf described him as lacking in the social graces. I described him as an ugly smelly foul-mouthed sneering git. He preyed on old people and the disabled in search of a fast buck and his very presence made me shudder. In short, with whatever respect is due, we did not want to act for him as he was rude, difficult and obnoxious. There is always one and he was it.

The police had charged him with five counts of deception, having taken money from old-age pensioners, promising to tarmac their drives then failing to turn up to do the work.

He was determined to plead not guilty and realising he needed to be represented he picked on me to do it. He was the one client in Rotherham who no one wanted to represent and unfortunately as the proceedings were in Rotherham I could not find a suitable excuse to duck the case.

He walked into my room, shrugged his shoulders and tossed gravy-stained charge sheets onto my desk.

"'ave these bastards," he said aggressively. "Not bastarding guilty to every bastard charge. I told the bastard police that I would 'ave done the work, but the bastards didn't give me chance, the bastards, just because they are bastard geriatrics and are getting ready to die they think they are entitled to special bastard privileges, the bastards, but they can bastard well think again, the bastards, so bastard well not guilty!"

I looked at the charge sheets and then at him and he snarled,

"They are a set of bastards."

"Do you really think so?" I asked.

"Bastards!"

"Quite….well Ray it seems that the police say you took £150 from each of the five elderly people as deposits, promising to do the work but they didn't get the work done."

"Bastards!"

"They don't appear to have had their deposits back."

"Bastards!"

"The deposits had been paid six months ago so the suggestion is that they had been ripped off, otherwise the work would have been done earlier than that."

"Bastards!"

"Were you going to do the work or not?"

"Bastards – of course I was but they couldn't wait, the bastards."

"How long were they supposed to wait?"

"Until I was bastard ready. Who do they think they are?"

I suppressed the desire to inject his private parts with Semtex and I accepted the challenge to get through the interview without losing my temper whilst continuing to remain pleasant and professional.

"If these old people give evidence and are believed, the court will be very upset with you and I think they will take a serious view as to your sentence."

"Fuck 'em!"

"Are you prepared to pay the deposits back?"

"No!"

"Why not?"

"Fuck 'em. I'll do the work when I can."

"Had you ordered the materials?"

"Didn't need to until I was ready. I wasn't ready so there was no intention to permanently deprive, so no dishonesty. It's a civil dispute not a criminal case, so fuck 'em."

Unfortunately he had an argument but the prosecution could rely on the fact that despite having taken deposits he had not ordered any materials or taken any steps to do the work. The other problem was that he had been drawing Social Security benefit for the whole of that period and the 'Lord Chief Justice', my friendly neighbourhood magistrate would love that. I could just image the cross-examination when my friend the Prosecutor Neil Franklin started putting him through the hoops.

Prosecutor: "And what do you think now of those old people who have lost their deposits?"

Turton: "Fuck 'em!"

Yes, I was right in thinking Turton would be found guilty so I set about telling him so.

"If you don't mind me saying so Ray old lad, you don't actually come over very well when you tell your story. Perhaps you could drop the swearing."

"For fuck's sake…."

"Exactly. You see, I don't think the magistrates will find your rather volatile range of expletives acceptable," I said hoping to make my point.

Ray looked at me, sneered and took a deep breath and we both spoke in unison,

"Fuck 'em."

There was no alternative, I had to try to get through to him one way or another.

"The problem is Ray that your manner leaves a lot to be desired."

"I didn't come 'ere to be insulted by you or any fucker."

"You just have been."

"Listen, no matter what they say I told them it would be at least six months before I started work because I was buying me tarmac in bulk and if they say different then fuck 'em."

"Well look, let's fill in your Legal Aid application and when I see the evidence I will advise you further."

"Yes, don't forget the Legal Aid application. When I think 'ow much Legal Aid money I've put your way, if it weren't for the likes of me you would be out of a job."

"I suppose you're right Ray. Just think, if I didn't have the delight of having to listen to your verbal shite, how could I face another day on God's earth?"

"Exactly," said a self-satisfied Ray Turton. "Now then, 'ave you got any fags?"

"No!"

"Mean bastard.   You ought to be supplying them to your best customers."

"Then you'd never get one," I said sarcastically.

"Anyway, I want my conditions of bail altering.   They say I can't go on Wickersley Road but I take my dog a walk down there so stopping me is not acceptable, get it?"

Oh, I had got it all right and how much I would like to have given it to him!

"I'll see you on Monday then," I said.

"Is that it?   What about taking a statement?"

"Wait until I see the evidence and then we'll do it and it will give me the delight óf seeing you again."

"Right," said Turton.

He finished picking his nose and then got up to move.

"Don't suppose you've got a drink in then?"

"Right again Ray, I haven't."

He grunted.   "You 'aven't got any sandwiches have you?"

"No, I'm afraid not."

"No, I suppose you eat out don't you?   Sandwiches will be no good to you.   Big three course meals and wine eh, followed by double brandies?"

"No Ray, just single brandies, they go better with the Château Neuf Du Pape."

"Huh," he mumbled under his breath, "Clever bastard."

"Well, I'll really look forward to seeing you again Ray, OK?"

"Fuck 'em!"

"Yes of course........oh and thank you."

Turton grunted again and walked out in search of an interview at the DSS and a crisis loan.

It was not difficult to see why everyone hated him; unfortunately he did not appear to have any good points at all.

Monica Jeffreys on the other hand was a gem. It is true she was a persistent shoplifter, but she was so easy to deal with, so courteous and charming, that after dealing with Turton seeing her was rather like an audience with Mother Theresa.

She entered my room very soon after Turton had left.

"Hello Mr Smith, it's nice to see you again."

"Hello Mrs Jeffreys. May I say how nice it is to see you."

Monica Jeffreys sat on the chair situated across from the leather topped desk. She was clean and tidy wearing a green tweed suit with matching shoes and a headscarf. She was sixty-five years old and a widow, who looked more like a friendly nun than Rotherham's greatest shoplifter but her façade of integrity was a mere mask, concealing the best pair of 'shoplifting hands' around.

Monica did not have a conviction until she was sixty but something seemed to draw her into dishonesty like a moth to a flame.

She was about five feet two inches tall, of slim build, had nicely kept iron grey hair and manicured hands, displaying a variety of expensive looking rings which according to Monica were fakes.

There could not be a greater contrast with Turton, for Monica was clean, tidy, well-spoken and as pleasant a person as you could wish to meet and Turton wasn't.

It was true that she never pleaded guilty, but it was equally true that she was rarely convicted. Unfortunately most of the Rotherham bench knew her, having acquitted her on so many occasions, but this was a classic example of someone whose manner and presentation were so respectful and friendly that magistrates hadn't the heart to convict her.

"Would you like a cup of tea Mrs Jeffreys?" I asked brightly.

"Oh wonderful, how thoughtful, yes I would please, and would you like a piece of cake or a scone?"

Monica had brought some baking in a rather splendid tin especially designed for the purpose, which she opened proudly to show a mixture of home-made cakes and her famous scones.

"I'm afraid there is only one scone left. Mr Wilford took one and Mr Jarvis the other. Mr Wilford likes a scone doesn't he?"

"Don't we all," I said as I inspected the left-overs.

I took two lemon tarts and began to eat them, exaggerating my reaction of pleasure to an anxious Mrs Jeffreys who lived for compliments about her baking.

"Wonderful, Mrs Jeffreys, what a fantastic taste, melts in the mouth and up to your usual high standard."

She giggled coyly – we had made her day. What a smashing client she was.

"I'll leave the tin and pick it up later in the week when I bring you a cake for the weekend."

"Really Mrs Jeffreys, you don't have to..........."

"Don't mention it, you're all so kind."

I was finding it hard to ask the purpose of her visit because quite simply I did not want to embarrass her but she saved me the problem.

"I'm afraid I've made another mistake," she said seriously.

"I was in the supermarket doing my shopping and I forgot to pay for a bottle of gin. I don't know how I forgot, but I just did, silly me.   What would I want with a bottle of gin?"

I had never seen Monica affected by drink before, so I suppose she could have been right, perhaps it was an error.

"I think you should plead not guilty at this stage," I said encouragingly.

"Do you really think so?" asked Monica.

"Yes, I'll check the evidence and we'll decide then."

"Oh good, does that mean you will want to see me again?"

"Certainly."

"Oh, how lovely!"

"Does that mean we'll be treated to more cake?"

"Certainly," she said proudly.

"Then we'll both be happy."

I completed the Legal Aid application but was feeling embarrassed to ask Monica for her financial details when she reached into her bag to bring out her widow's pension book and a copy of her building society account.

She was in receipt of the grand sum of £47 per week and had just over £100 in savings.   I couldn't help but feel so sorry for her because she was a lonely old lady and I was convinced she shoplifted for a reason other than to get away without paying.

We talked for over an hour about her life in service up to the time when she met Herbert, to whom she was married for forty-five years until he died from a massive stroke.

"I still miss him," said Monica thoughtfully as her eyes moistened over.   "Oh listen to silly me, feeling sorry for myself again.   Anyway, what about your family, are they all right?"

"Yes they are, thank you."

"Oh good, it's nice when families stay together."

"Yes it is. Tell me Mrs Jeffreys, remind me, did you have any children?"

She didn't answer straightaway. But then:

"Yes, I had a son but he died shortly after Herbert.........it was an accident........"

Monica was deep in thought as if my question had taken some remembering. She appeared in the course of the next few seconds to re-live those terrible events and how I wished I hadn't asked the question.

She continued as though there had been no pause.

"Fortunately he didn't feel a thing.......it was over in an instant.........a supermarket lorry knocked him off his bike and that was it.............Geoffrey was a good boy, clever like his father...........good worker too.............."

The pauses between the sentences became longer.

"He never had a chance.............the driver never looked.................too keen to get his delivery made on time for fear of being told off................but look at the consequences.........he was my only child"

I changed the subject realising I had caused her distress. After having suffered a foul-mouthed Turton the circumstances had turned full circle and now I was consoling a nice person who wasn't really harming anyone, except perhaps the supermarkets.

Monica left the office highly delighted with the appreciation shown to her for her baking and it was clear she had had her hair done especially for the appointment which had been the highlight of her day, but yet when she had gone I was struck by a strange melancholia.

Wilf broke the silence.

"Nice old lady, Mrs Jeffreys."

"Yes, she is," I replied thoughtfully.

"Nice buns.   She's baking us a cake for the weekend."

"Yes, she is," I replied again.

"Been shoplifting has she?"

"Yes, she has."

Just then it struck me.   I read the charge sheet – "Vernons Quick Sales," I muttered.

"You what?" asked Wilf, confused, thinking I had been speaking to him.

"Vernons Quick Sales," I replied triumphantly, "I wonder if...............?"

"Wonder what?"

"Oh, nothing.   It's just an idea......about Monica."

"You're not making any sense said Wilf, clearly confused.

"I'll tell you when I know more.   Of course I could be wrong, but something tells me......."

"What the bloody hell are you talking about?" asked Wilf impatiently.

"I'll tell you later."

Wilf picked up the remnants of my scone and ate it. "She's a bloody good baker even if she is a tea leaf," he said and walked back to his room.

I gathered all my papers together with a view to leaving, when the telephone rang and I deliberated as to whether to answer it, but my curiosity got the better of me.

"It's the police station," said Tracey.   "Albert's locked up. The police have arrested him in possession of two sheep and he says they were lost."

I took a deep breath and mumbled to myself,

"What now?"

The Rotherham police station was a custom-built building, fairly new with all the latest equipment and mod cons, thumbscrews, torture chambers etc and a dying breed of officers who believed things were better in their day. It was a short walk away from my office and on my arrival I was taken to the cell area to look through the spy-hole in the cell door where I saw Albert sitting with his back to the wall. He looked less than pleased as the sergeant opened the large steel door, but I walked inside to find that at least Albert was pleased to see me.

"Thank God you're 'ere Steve, this is a right cock-up!"

I was used to all sorts of stories and excuses and over the years I regret I had become quite cynical but in Albert's case, when he was guilty, there was usually a large grin across his face. On this occasion he was stern and serious.

"What's happened Albert?" I asked.

"I've not nicked two sheep."

"Well, according to what the police suggest, they found you walking through the park in Rotherham with two sheep on a lead made out of rope."

"That's true, yes I was."

"The police say that the sheep belonged to a farm not far away."

"That's true, yes."

"They say that the sheep were some distance from the farm and you were walking in the opposite direction to it."

"That's true, that's right," said Albert.

They also say that the owner of the sheep says that no one has any right to take them off his land."

"That's right, yes that's right."

"In short Albert, they say that they were rustled and they were rustled by you."

"That's not right."

"Well, what's happened then?"

"I've told 'em what's 'appened. It's dead easy. I was on my way 'ome and they were on the main road. They'd obviously got out and got lost and they were panicking. I know, because I understand animals."

"Yes, I know you do Albert."

"There were cars swerving round 'em, blowing their 'orns and frightening them to death, so I got a piece of rope and made a lead. I was near the park so I thought it would calm them down if I took them in and they could eat some grass or summat like that and I would wander back 'ome with them, just to try to calm them down, and then we'd get the van out and try and find where they came from. They'd got a mark on their fur which should show which farm they belong to; it's like an identification mark."

"Why didn't you take them back there and then?" I asked.

"Because I didn't know where they came from and there's no farm that close to the park, it looked like a transport job. Not only that, 'ave you ever tried taking two sheep on a lead? If they don't want to go, they let you know about it."

I realised that not only did he have a reasonable story, but he may well have been telling the truth.

I considered the various options. I did not believe that Albert would have killed the animals for meat or anything like that because of his love for animals. He would not have sold them to anyone else for that purpose and he certainly wouldn't want them as pets, so I was drawn to the view that he must be telling the truth.

"The police will want to interview you about this Albert."

"They can interview me for as long as they want, I 'aven't rustled these sheep."

I called the police in and we went into interview where Albert maintained his story very forcefully indeed.

There wasn't really much evidence other than he'd got two sheep in his possession which didn't belong to him and his account was satisfactory so the police were therefore in difficulties so far as charging him was concerned.

I spoke to the custody sergeant who decided that Albert would be released on police bail to allow them to make further enquiries, and I went back to the cell area to advise Albert that he was going to be bailed. He was relieved.

"I don't mind being done for summat I've done, but I'm not getting' done for summat I've not done."

"Fair comment Albert," I said, "Fair comment, but I don't think you're going to be done for this. Your explanation is very satisfactory and they've really no evidence to contradict it, so with a bit of luck when you come back on your police bail I don't think there'll be a charge."

"OK," said Albert, "'ow about a lift 'ome?"

Within a fairly short time Albert was released from the cells and I gave him a lift home, but not before I'd had a long conversation with the sergeant as to how the sheep were going to get back to the farm.

"I'll take them back if you want?" said Albert

"Not bloody likely," said the custody sergeant. "That got you in this mess in the first place."

"Why don't you just leave them in the compound and the owner will come and fetch them?" I suggested.

"Well, you ought to give them some water," said Albert, "'cos when they're under stress they like water."

The sergeant was not impressed at being given orders.

"How the bloody hell do you know, you're not a vet are you?"

"He's not far off," I said. "When it comes to animals there's not much you can tell him."

"Right then Buffalo Bill," said the sergeant, "This time you're going to be bailed. You've been bailed for a fortnight and I have to tell you that if you don't come back in a fortnight you commit an offence because you're in breach of bail. Got it?"

Got it," said Albert

"Very good," said the sergeant.

I took Albert home and for once I actually believed he was innocent.

"You do believe me Steve, don't you?"

"Yes I do as a matter of fact Albert. I can't understand this change that's come over you. You seem to have calmed down. Perhaps it's your liaison with Caroline."

"My what with Caroline?"

"Your association I mean."

"My association?"

"Yes, you going out with her I mean."

"Oh, well I like my job, and they said that if I got into trouble again they would sack me."

"Do you enjoy working at the Animal Sanctuary Albert?"

"Ay, it's great."

I realised that Albert was better at getting on with animals than he was with human beings and he certainly had an incredible rapport with animals of all descriptions.

I dropped him off at his home and he waved as I drove off.

Fourteen days later Albert returned to the police station and the charges were dropped, but he did get a thank-you note from the farmer.

The next morning's court was uneventful until I met Granville Wolstenholme who had been prosecuted for cutting down trees which were the subject of a Tree Preservation Order. The local council had prosecuted him and there he was before the Magistrates Court for offences which attracted some very substantial fines.

Mr Wolstenholme was a peculiar character and amongst other things suffered from a nervous twitch which had the effect of an extremely quick movement of the head from right to left and back again. The head moved with such speed that his face was a blur during the movement and how on earth he didn't become dizzy at the completion of the manoeuvre was a wonder to me.

I was later to find out that he had suffered from this problem since he was at school, where he had answered to the rather cruel nickname of Granville Twitchit.

The emphysemic usher introduced me to him at his request and I took him into the rathole interview room where we sat opposite each other at the makeshift desk.

"I've come to see you about these charges Mr Smith and I rather hope that you will represent me." With that he performed one of his violent manoeuvres which held me spellbound.

"There are five charges in all which are to be prosecuted by the local council and I wish to be advised on the merits of a not guilty plea." With that, another violent twitch which regrettably but unavoidably left me rather open-mouthed.

"The council have prosecuted my wife as well, in respect of the same five trees. In fairness she had nothing to do with it," and with that his head set off again.

"Who represents your wife?" I asked him politely.

"I hope you will," said Mr Wolstenholme, "But she must plead not guilty for it was nothing to do with her." With that he twitched again.

"Well, I think the best thing I can do is to take some basic details now and then adjourn the case to see the evidence after which we can meet in the office where I will probably be in a better position to advise you both. Would you like to bring your wife in to see me?"

"She's not here today because unfortunately she is ill, but I understand that because she is on Summons and not bail there is no need for her to attend if the case is being adjourned."

He was right and consequently I took the opportunity of adjourning the case, on the basis that I needed to see the evidence so we could decide what pleas to enter.

As Mr Wolstenholme was leaving he offered his hand to shake which prompted two violent twitches instead of the usual one, and I could feel the shock waves running from his neck, down his arm into my hand, which prompted my profound sympathy for him in his unfortunate affliction.

I took Mr Wolstenholme into court and managed to get the case called on early. The Council's solicitor was a fairly pleasant fellow who was just doing his job and was not in for blood, so I managed to get the case adjourned for four weeks, which gave me plenty of time to see both clients to sort the case out.

During the adjournment I arranged for them both to call in and see me and it was to be an experience I would never forget.

Mrs Wolstenholme was a sharp-nosed middle-aged lady, very slim and small of stature. She had short-cropped grey curly hair with a tuft at the front which appeared to have been forgotten during the brushing process, because it stuck up rather like that of a Mohawk Indian and when she moved her head it waved from side to side, tempting you to

wave back.   I have no idea why, but I could not help but
focus my attention upon it whilst I was speaking to her.
Mr Wolstenholme sat down and flicked his head from side
to side in the usual way, with a considerable flourish
"This is my wife Agnes, Mr Smith," he said, "But you can
call her Mrs Wolstenholme."
He did not appear to be joking.
I held out my hand to shake hers and in doing so and much
to my surprise, she twitched her head from side to side, but
in the opposite direction to that which served her husband.
I was left rather in shock as Mr Wolstenholme began to
speak and repeat very much what he had told me before
about his case.   I must admit I was not taking it in as I was
still reeling under the sight of this husband and wife team,
both of whom were similarly afflicted.
"Pass Mr Smith your summons Agnes," and with that he
twitched again.
"Certainly Granville.   I'm afraid one of them has been
torn, but they are still legible," she said twitching from
right to left.
Sooner or later they were bound to twitch simultaneously
and if it happened whilst they were drinking tea I would
not have known how to deal with it; however the tea
arrived and to my considerable regret the cups had been
placed on saucers so they would be even more precarious
at 'twitch time'.   It seemed that the more stressed they
became whilst relaying the story, the more likely the twitch
was to take place, so I did my very best to try to put them
at their ease and this appeared to work until I mentioned
the charges which prompted a twitch from each of them,
although it was far from synchronised.

We went through the evidence and it seemed fairly clear that the responsibility for the felling of the trees lay at Mr Wolstenholme's door with his wife a passive observer. It was true that the house was in joint names but I felt the prosecution against her was weak.

"This may be a case Mr Wolstenholme where if I told the Prosecution that you are prepared to plead guilty, they may drop the charges against your wife."

The reference to the charges prompted twitching from them both, causing the teacups to wobble on their saucers.

"If the Prosecution are prepared to do that," said Mr Wolstenholme, "Then I will plead Guilty. I really don't want to see Agnes charged."

The magic word 'charge' prompted yet another violent twitch causing the teacup to wobble quite precariously in its saucer, but the amazing thing was that both Mr & Mrs Wolstenholme appeared to be oblivious to their ailments.

Just then there was a knock on the door and in walked Wilf who was looking for a book of precedents, so as a matter of courtesy I introduced him to my clients who stood up in turn to shake hands when each of them provided us with a glorious twitch. The look on Wilf's face was a joy to behold as Mr & Mrs Wolstenholme sat down and as he was leaving the office, Wilf looked at me with a puzzled gaze, so I looked back in a threatening way in the hope that he didn't embarrass me with a quick twitch of his own.

Mr Wolstenholme continued the conversation.

"You may have noticed Mr Smith that I have a health problem."

"Oh, I hadn't really noticed," I said trying to be polite.

"Oh yes, in fact many people tell me it's quite noticeable. You see I have a bad back and I walk with a slight stoop."

"Oh yes, of course," I said, "I see what you mean."

"This means that I am not always able to clear up the garden, particularly in autumn when the leaves fall. In addition, all the branches on these trees are cutting out the light, so it's vital that I chop them down. I knew that there was some kind of Order on the trees but I didn't think it was so important. What I can't understand is how the Council got to know about it?"

"Well you have neighbours and the sound of chainsaws would obviously draw attention to what was going on, so any passer-by could have seen it I suppose."

"Yes, I suppose that's true. I rather suspected it was someone with a grudge."

"Have you crossed swords with any of your neighbours?" I asked.

"I thought I got on with them quite well," said Mr Wolstenholme, twitching violently from right to left.

Throughout the whole of this conversation his wife had been watching him most carefully and could not have possibly missed the violent twitching, but perhaps she had become accustomed to it so didn't really notice it as being anything out of the ordinary.

Just then the telephone rang and I was told that Sean Page was waiting for me in reception. I had forgotten that I had arranged to go out with him at lunchtime and it was now ten minutes to one. I told Tracey that I would be out within the next few minutes and as I continued to take details I could hear Pagey's raucous laughter from the reception area.

A feeling of impending doom came into my mind as I realised that the two Wolstenholme's would have to walk through the reception area to the exit. Inevitably they would walk past Pagey or even worse, meet him, and I shuddered to think what his reaction might be.

When I concluded our conversation I was about to get up to show them out when an insect flew past me, causing me to move my head rapidly almost in a twitching fashion. I felt considerable embarrassment and the need to explain what I had done, which I suppose would have appeared most peculiar to my guests.

We walked out into the reception area where Pagey greeted me.

"Good day old bean, are we ready?"

"Certainly Sean."

Pagey had got out of his chair and manners decreed that I should introduce him to the Wolstenholmes, although my heart was beating and my mind racing for fear that I should cause any offence but then my worst nightmare came true. Because I had concentrated so greatly upon their ailments, in a Freudian slip I very foolishly introduced my clients as Mr and Mrs Twitchett which led to simultaneous twitching.

Pagey thought it was some form of joke and so in his usual way he entered into the spirit of the occasion.

"Aptly named, what?" said Pagey twitching in an exaggerated fashion.

Mrs Wolstenholme screwed up her face in annoyance.

"Nice to have met you," said Pagey, twitching violently with his head and holding his thumb up into the air.

Mr & Mrs Wolstenholme were appalled and set off down the stairs without speaking.

"I say," said Pagey, "Have I said something out of order?"

I shook my head but didn't speak.

"Funny couple, what? I thought it was a big joke, Mr Noddy and Mrs Noddy. Well some people just can't take a joke."

With that we set off for the Cross Keys and Harold's famous steak pie.

Ray Turton's case came up quite quickly and he entered Not Guilty pleas with a sneer which meant that the Prosecution would have to call all the old people he had duped, to give evidence. In cases where you have vulnerable complainants the court loses any sympathy they might have for the defendant, but Ray was disinterested to the point of contempt.

"He's a very unpleasant fellow," said the emphysemic usher.

I nodded my agreement.

"He was very rude to me when I called out his name."

"He's very rude to everybody," I replied wearily. "In fact, he's just about the most ignorant man I've ever met in my life."

"I'm glad you think so," said the emphysemic usher. "I thought it was just me."

Turton had pleaded Not Guilty and the case was adjourned for a Trial to take place the following month. This was a Trial I didn't want and to be perfectly frank I was living in hope that Turton would sack me and pick on somebody else, but in the event, he didn't.

The following day Mrs Jeffries appeared before the court to enter her plea, when politely and rather demurely she spoke the words "Not Guilty" and subsequently was allowed to sit in the dock whilst the court clerk obtained a convenient date for the trial from his Listing Officer. Whilst we were waiting Neil Franklin, the Prosecutor,

214

showed me her criminal record, on which were three previous convictions for theft, all for shoplifting, and her last conviction was approximately six months before, although she had been acquitted of a number of other charges in the past. Out of the ten occasions she had appeared in court she had only been convicted three times, which I suppose was pretty good odds.

The criminal record usually gives the dates of the offences with the date and place of conviction, but it doesn't usually give the name of the premises where the theft occurred. However on this occasion, inexplicably, the last conviction did mention it - it was an offence at Vernons Quick Sales.

"What an unusual coincidence I thought to myself. The current charge involved an offence at Vernons and her last conviction was at the same place."

I couldn't help wondering where the other convictions were but then my considerations were interrupted by Keith Copley, the Court Clerk, who told us that the Listing Officer had no convenient dates within the next eight weeks and so he decided to let the Bench retire, when he would go to the office himself to sort the matter out. It meant a short retirement so we were able to visit the WRVS tea-room for a traditional cup of enamel remover.

I used the adjournment period to see my friend Inspector George Swift of Prosecutions, who was a thirty-year man about to retire and who during the course of his duties had more or less seen it all. The conviction card had a reference number for the other entries and out of interest I asked him if it were possible to turn up those old files to see where the offences had been committed.

George was in a good mood and said that he would check, although it would take half an hour or so for the police cadet assigned to his office to do the running about.

"I'm sorry to put you to this trouble, George," I said. "If it's going to involve a lot of work, please don't bother."

"No, I don't mind and it'll let young Peter here gain some experience of looking up files," he said, referring to a lanky youth with a poor complexion.

He turned to the cadet, who looked as though he could do with seven or eight hot dinners, preferably all on one day, gave him his instructions and Peter set off as though his life depended upon it whilst I picked up a pear from George's desk.

"You can put that down, that's part of my dinner….healthy eating, that's the order of the day and my new diet."

I put the pear back on his desk and he took it away, almost as if he thought there was a possibility of me trying to lift it again.

I went back into court and finished the rest of my work, only to receive a message from the police cadet about a half-hour later, which concerned Monica Jeffries and confirmed my suspicion; namely that each of her convictions related to offences at Vernons Quick Sales. I put the note down on the desk to think for a moment and I was so deep in thought I must actually have spoken out loud because Neil Franklin replied.

"So that's what Smithy?" he asked.

His comments seemed to awaken me from my deliberations.

"That's what?" I asked.

"You must be losing it Smithy, you just said to me 'so that's it' so I'm asking you what is it?"

"Oh, it's nothing, it's just about a case."

I got up to go and Franklin looked at me rather blankly, shrugging his shoulders as if to imply that my thought processes had failed to function.

When I got outside Mrs Jeffries was waiting for me, so I took her to the rathole interview room and sat her down, where armed with two cups of enamel remover plus two custard creams I opened up her file.

"Mrs Jeffries?" I asked contemplatively.

"Yes, what is it?"

"Do you mind if I ask you about your past history?"

"Yes, of course. I'm sorry, it's not something to be proud of, but I hadn't done it and the court found me guilty on each of the three occasions.   It seems that the court preferred the evidence of Vernon's rather than mine."

I didn't embarrass her by saying that they believed her on seven other occasions because I didn't wish to create a conflict between us, and in any case I had considerable sympathy for the old girl.

"According to the records, each of these convictions was at Vernon's."

Mrs Jeffries paused for a minute and looked almost as if she had been caught out.

"Yes, they were at Vernon's."

"Was there any particular reason for that?"

"No," she said, but she was clearly embarrassed.   "Not really, it's just a coincidence."

She stammered as she spoke and if I needed a clue, that was it.

We agreed to meet at the office shortly before the Trial to go through the evidence so that events would be fresh in

Monica's mind, although she seemed troubled on this occasion as we parted.

I could not get Monica Jeffries out of my mind. I never really thought, despite her convictions and her acquittals, that she was a thief, because it seemed incongruous that a lady such as this should involve herself in dishonesty. After all, whilst she was not well off she was not destitute, did not need to steal to survive and dishonesty was not in her nature. I had, of course, come across old ladies who stole just for the thrill of it, although I did not accept any of these theories as her motivation, but then an idea struck me.

I really needed some professional advice to confirm my theory so my next port of call was the psychiatrist's chair as soon as the opportunity presented itself. I would not have long to wait.

Chapter Thirteen

Monica's Revenge

On the Friday night of that week I attended the Chartered Accountants' Dinner as the guest of Michael Jarvis, and I was sitting with him, Chris Good and Tenbelly Norburn. During the interval, before the speeches, I went to the bar to secure four glasses of lemonade or something similar when I bumped into an old friend of mine called Neville Gittlestone, a Consultant Psychiatrist from Sheffield, who had been a doctor for many years and specialising in psychiatry. It was my lucky day and I told him so.

We struck up a conversation during which I decided to broach the subject of Monica Jeffries, giving him the background and saying that my main concern was her motivation for crime. I told him about her son's accident and Neville's eyes lit up in recognition.

"It's an interesting case," said Neville thoughtfully. "I've come across this sort of thing before. You say that she is a widow?"

"Yes, she lost her husband and then shortly afterwards her son. It must have been a terrific jolt to her."

"Yes, of course. Tell me what happened."

"Well, her husband died of a heart attack without warning and her son was killed in a road accident, being on his pedal cycle when he was run over by a Vernon's delivery van. It was the van driver's fault and Mrs Jeffries was devasted".

"Your client is suffering from a depressive disorder, brought on I've no doubt by the background of upset. It usually takes the form of exhibitionism and the desire to be noticed and it's a rather complex way of showing an emotional response or reaction to the pain that she has suffered.   In short, it is a classic grief-type reaction."

"What can be done about it?"

"She needs psychiatric help before it consumes her; before it gets totally out of control."

"You mean, it could go a little further than just shoplifting?"

"Well there's always the possibility and you can't exclude that the revenge factor might prompt her to take even greater sanction against the firm."

"My problem is in persuading her that she needs psychiatric help.   My experience of people, certainly in that age-group, is that they are not enlightened to matters of psychiatry and she may well feel that I'm suggesting that she is mad."

"Well, the best way is to allow her to plead guilty to the offence, then tell the court what the difficulties are and get them to order psychiatric reports.   That way she has no option and then we can see her to formulate a proper report, which could be given to the Probation Service who could then compile their own report suggesting a Probation Order, possibly with a condition of treatment."

"It is treatable then?"

"Oh yes, certainly," said the good doctor, but it needs to be addressed now rather than later.

"It wouldn't involve going into hospital, would it?"

"No, it can be done on an out-patients basis, but subject to her condition it might need a very short assessment in hospital, but I see no reason why she should need to be made an in-patient."

"There is a major difficulty."

"Oh, what's that?"

"Well, she always pleads not guilty and based on what you say, she could be trying to inconvenience the store by having them all attend court."

"Yes, you could see it that way, but can't you advise her to plead guilty?"

"Yes, I certainly can advise her to do so, but whilst she maintains her innocence it's not for me to tell her that she's guilty. It's the most common question I'm asked, namely 'how can you represent someone that you know is guilty?' My belief does not enter into it. For example, I might be wrong."

"But in this case you're not wrong, she has done it."

"Well, that's my belief, although she's denied it to the police and told them that it's just a question of forgetfulness."

"What did she steal?"

"It was some electrical item, not worth an awful lot but it puts the store to a great deal of inconvenience."

"Is there a prospect that she might get away with it?"

"Well there's always a prospect that she might be acquitted and what do I do then?"

"Well, if she's found not guilty the court has no sanction to order reports. You cannot order psychiatric reports upon someone who's been found not guilty can you?"

"I suppose not."

We were interrupted by the speeches, but in the bar afterwards we continued our discussion.

"It seems an interesting case," said the doctor.

"Oh, it's an interesting case all right but my concern is for her. I think the only way I can deal with this is to grasp the nettle and confront her with it."

"Yes by all means, but you should do it as delicately as you can, otherwise she may well see you as part and parcel of the opposition. My advice to you is that you be seen to be her friend."

"Of course."

The following day I went to the library to familiarise myself with the subject as best I could. The problem was simple: I had to persuade Mrs Jeffries to plead guilty and then get her to see a psychiatrist, but it wasn't going to be easy.

I wrote to her and asked her to visit me later that week when sure enough she came in with her customary cake and scones which were handed around the office until everyone was satisfied except me as there were none left, so as usual I missed out. We talked briefly for a few minutes as I gently set the scene.

"What worries me most Mrs Jeffries is your health. You have had some terrible times to face."

"Yes, I know, but I'm doing my best."

"I know you are, but sometimes we don't realise that we are ill and sometimes we won't face it either."

"I know what you mean," said Mrs Jeffries, and I was heartened at the advance I had made.

"I remember one case I did for someone who had faced tragedies like you and they got very, very depressed."

"Yes, they would do," said Mrs Jeffries.

"In fact they were so depressed that they became very ill indeed and I got so worried about them I even had to call in a psychiatrist," I said, having taken a deep breath.

Mrs Jeffries' hitherto co-operative demeanour seemed to cease. It was almost as if she realised what I was building up to, and then my worst fears were realised.

222

"There's nothing wrong with me that requires a psychiatrist. I'm not mad you know……In fact, you think I'm mad…….I'm sure you do……..but I'm not I tell you."
The outburst was more or less what I expected.
"Of course I don't think that you're mad. What you've got to understand is that some people think that all psychiatrists do is deal with mad people. Nothing could be further from the truth. They are very good at dealing with depression as well."
"I'm a bit down, but I'm not depressed and I certainly don't need a psychiatrist," shouted Monica.
"I'm not suggesting you do Mrs Jeffries, all I'm saying is that sometimes we can be very depressed without really knowing it and it causes us to do all sorts of things," I said, trying to placate her.
"Oh, I see what you're getting at now. You think I'm some form of kleptomaniac."
I tried to laugh off the suggestion.
"Nothing could be further from the truth, but I know it is a fact that you have had a terrible time."
"We all know that," said Mrs Jeffries, "But I don't need to be carted off to the looney-bin."
"Well I'm not pushing it, it was just a thought as I'm genuinely concerned about your health. I'm only thinking about your welfare."
"Well thank you very much, I'm sure you mean it for the best, but this was a genuine mistake and I am pleading not guilty."
"Yes, of course you are," I said, realising that I'd probably gone a little too far. "Don't worry, we'll talk again later."
"Not about pleading guilty and not about psychiatrists," she said firmly.

223

I thought that if the Magistrates found her guilty I would let the court order reports and she wouldn't have any say in the matter, but there was a time to back off and this was it. I decided to fight another day and Mrs Jeffries left in reasonable spirits, but a little disgruntled.

The day of the Trial soon arrived and it was a case which I was dreading, as I have rarely ever been so concerned about a Defendant as I was in this case. Her instructions were to fight the case on the basis that it was not theft but a mistake and so it was to be a trial with all witnesses present to give evidence. She arrived at court in a very smart tweed suit but I noticed that she had lost some weight and the jacket had become ill-fitting. Nevertheless she still looked smart, with her hair done and her nails beautifully manicured, looking the epitome of everyone's favourite grandmother.

The Prosecutor opened his case and told the Magistrates that he was suggesting that this was no mistake, but a deliberate attempt to steal, a view supported by the store detective who gave her evidence, emphasising that before Mrs Jeffries put the bottle of gin into her bag she looked around her surreptitiously which caused the store detective to concentrate on what she was doing. She was then said to have collected a number of items which she placed into a shopping trolley.

Monica was followed to the check-out where she presented all the items for payment except the gin, which remained in her shopping bag, so of course when she'd walked through the check-out without paying, the store detective apprehended her and took her to the manager's office.

The Prosecutor asked his questions in such a way as to try to discount entirely the question of mistake.

"You say that Mrs Jeffries looked around surreptitiously. Could you explain what you mean?" he asked.

"Yes, it was as if she was looking to see if anyone was watching her. She had not seen me because I was at the bottom of the aisle, peering around the shelves," replied the store detective.

"Are you in any doubt as to what you saw?"

"No, I'm not."

It was then my turn to cross-examine her but before I spoke I looked towards Monica, a desolate figure sitting all alone in the massive dock.

"You say you were down at the bottom of the aisle?"

"Yes, that is correct."

"How far away from Mrs Jeffries were you at the time?"

"I would say almost the full length of the store, some sixty feet or so."

"And you had a clear view?"

"Yes, I did."

"You say that you were peering around some shelves. Was that at the end of the row?"

"Yes, it was."

"When you say you were peering, what do you mean?"

"Well, it was just part of my head, enough for me to be able to see."

"So you would be sticking your head out?"

"Well yes, but only just."

"But you must have stuck your head out, otherwise you wouldn't have been able to see?"

"Well, I suppose that's right."

"If you had been standing in Mrs Jeffries' place, do you think you would have been able to have seen what you did?"

"Well I can't speak for Mrs Jeffries."

"I didn't ask you to speak for Mrs Jeffries, I simply asked you if you could have seen your head, so to speak?"

"Well yes, I suppose I could."

"When you say she was looking around surreptitiously, how long was she doing that for?"

"Oh, a second or two, that's all. I got the impression she was looking to see if anybody was watching," the detective said smugly.

"Well she didn't see you did she?"

"Well of course I can't speak for her, can I?" she replied even more smugly.

"Wasn't it a question of she was looking round, deep in thought, because what she will say is that she had forgotten what else she wanted. She was simply looking round at the shelves in an attempt to jog her memory as to what else she needed."

The store detective thought for a moment.

"I didn't think she was looking for somebody."

"But did she look in the direction of the shelves?"

"No, not at all."

"But she must have done, because if she was in the aisle and she was looking one way and then the other she must have been looking at the shelves surely?"

The store detective was beginning to look uncomfortable and was nowhere near as confident as when she first gave evidence.

"Well, I suppose she must have seen the shelves?"

"Exactly, that's what I've just been saying, so don't you think that it's possible she was looking for some*thing* as opposed to some*body*?"

There was a long pause before the store detective answered.

"No, I don't.   I think she was looking around to see if anyone had seen her."

"Well if you are so confident, can you tell me why it took you so long to answer?"

"Well, I was just thinking about what you said."

"So you had to think about it before you answered?"

"Well I suppose so."

"What was her behaviour at the check-out?"

"Quite normal.   She just put her items down for payment."

"Can you remember where her purse was?"

"No, I can't."

Would you accept from me that her purse was in her hand and she didn't have to open her bag to get to it?"

"I don't know, but I'll accept that if you wish."

"The point I'm making is that at no time at the till did she have cause to look into her shopping bag."

"I suppose so," said the store detective.

"So you would agree then that at no time at the check-out did she look into her shopping bag?"

"Yes, I would agree."

"And is it not right that the items which she purchased were placed into a carrier bag by an assistant at the check-out?"

The store detective thought for a moment in anticipation of what I was getting at and I showed a little of my impatience by prompting her to answer quickly.

"I can't remember," said the store detective.

"Well, are you prepared to accept that that was right, or not?"

"Yes, I accept that."

"So at no time, either at the check-out or shortly after, did she have cause to look into her bag?"

"Yes, that's correct," said the store detective with a sigh.

"It's right that she expressed surprise when you stopped her, isn't it?"

"Yes, she did.

"In fact, is it not right that she appeared to be very confused and actually told you that she didn't know what you meant when you asked her if she had something for which she'd not paid?

"Well, I suppose that's right yes, but that was part of her act."

"What do you mean by that?"

"Well, I mean she had stolen it hadn't she, so she'd got to look surprised?"

"Yes, but equally it could have been a genuine mistake, in which case she would have acted in a surprised manner, wouldn't she?"

The store detective did not answer so I continued.

"When the police came and you told them what you'd seen she said that she couldn't remember putting the item into the bag, that's true isn't it?"

"Yes, that's true."

"Isn't it right that she told the police officer that she had had no reason to look into her shopping bag?"

"Yes."

"And also that had she done so, she would have seen the gin and she would have immediately offered it for payment?"

There was no answer so I insisted.

"Isn't that right?"

"Yes, she did say that," said the store detective.

"But of course, as you say, you can't speak for what was in her mind can you?"

"Well, no," said the store detective.

I looked at the Magistrates and told them I had no further questions. I had the scent of blood and regardless of my initial view, I knew the case was going my way.

The police officer came in and simply confirmed what I had said, going even further when he told the court that Mrs Jeffries appeared to be genuinely upset. The Prosecutor tried to suggest that she was upset because she had been caught but the point had registered with the Magistrates and so I did not object to what he had said.

My trump card was actually calling Monica to give evidence and what a brilliant job she made of it. She came over as a kindly, honest but perhaps slightly confused old lady, who shouldn't really be in court.

The Bench retired after I had addressed them, suggesting that this was a daft thing to do but a genuine error. I asked them to put themselves in this lady's position and see how they would react in a store if they'd made a genuine error. I also asked them to take account of the fact that the trauma of the loss of her husband and her son may well leave her in a very confused state and should therefore this little old lady be convicted, following the humiliation of an arrest and an appearance at the police station in a cell?

The Magistrates retired for about ten minutes and then returned into the court. The Chairman announced his decision.

"We find you not guilty of this charge, Mrs Jeffries. You really must be more careful when you enter shops."

I had never felt so disappointed at winning a case.

She smiled sweetly, thanked the Magistrates and then left the court.

The Prosecutor smiled cynically before telling me,

"They wouldn't have thought she was so sweet if they'd seen her record."

I leaned across to him and in a whisper said,

"Everyone makes mistakes."

The Prosecutor pulled a face which showed his dissatisfaction and I winked at him and left for court, thanking the Magistrates as I did so.

I saw Monica outside and she was delighted, but the reality was that I would not be able to secure the psychiatric report that I needed. It was only a matter of time before she would be back and I wouldn't have long to wait.

Chapter Fourteen

All's Well That Ends..........

When I got back to the office I found my room occupied which left me nowhere to sit and dictate. I was annoyed at being inconvenienced and realised that we needed another floor at least so the only thing for it was to flit. We had to find somewhere else and I walked into Wilf's room to announce my idea.

"I haven't got anywhere to sit!" I said forcefully.

"Hmmmm," muttered Wilf.

"I said, I haven't got anywhere to sit!"

Wilf looked up from his papers.

"You want a what?"

"I said ......haven't you listened to a word........?"

"Not really," said Wilf as he put down his pen. "What's up?"

"You see, I haven't got a room, everywhere is full, we ought to have an articled clerk to help with the work but if we take anybody else on we simply have nowhere to put them. We've got to make a decision, either we stay where we are and shrink or we've got to expand. We need some more money to come in to deal with the overdraft and that means we'll have to take more work on."

"I can't take any more work on," Wilf said, "I'm up to my eyes in it as it is."

"Then we need some other staff."

"Well, I suppose we could use somebody but there's always the problem of another mouth to feed and then we'll need a new secretary."

"Exactly. That's what I mean," I said, "And where are we going to put them?"

After a long discussion we decided that the time had come for us to move on into larger premises, 11A Vicarage Lane had served its purpose but it was time to move, but to where? There was no real shortage of property in Rotherham but we needed to stay in the town centre so later that day Wilf brought in the weekly paper and there on the property page was an advertisement which stated 'Prestige Office for sale'. The address was 22 Westgate, formerly the offices of the Halifax Building Society, and we decided to take a look the following day.

The offices were marble-fronted with four floors and an exceptional basement. Floors two and three were open plan so they would need to be sectioned off whilst floor four would be ideal for overspill.

It was in the town centre, close to the banks, building societies, the courts and the Cross Keys. It was perfect although it would cost a lot of money to heat, but somehow the expense did not seem to matter and we would be buying not renting, so one day it would be ours – when the mortgage had been paid.

I must confess to a sense of remarkable excitement and we were just like schoolboys receiving their first football. We wanted to get our bid in straight away and with Wilf sorting out the conveyancing all looked well.

Our offer was accepted the following week and with completion set for the New Year we looked forward to a new chapter in the story of Wilford Smith & Co. In the meantime life carried on much as it had before, except for FiFi Dupont whom I ran into on my way to court early one morning. I was quite surprised to see her and indeed at first I didn't recognise her at all, such was the change. Her hair was back to its normal colour, her skirt was to the knee and she was wearing about a quarter of the make-up that she usually daubed onto her face.

"I didn't recognise you at first, you've changed," I said, opening the conversation.

"Yes, everybody says that, it's perhaps a good idea that nobody can recognise me."

"What's brought this on then?" I asked.

"Well, I've decided that it was time I should grow up. I am going to plead guilty to that charge and get it over with. I thought you might be interested to know I've got a job now."

"Really, what are you doing?

"I'm working at an old folks' home as a care assistant. It's a long story how I came to get the job but they've put me on three months trial and to be honest with you, I'm really enjoying it."

I was delighted and told her so.

"I've decided I'm going to sit the social worker exams and so I've enrolled at the college. I've moved from my old place and I'm now in the new flats just outside of town."

I took a note of her new address and told her how impressed I was with her efforts. I was satisfied she was genuine. When we got to court the following week the Magistrates were also impressed and they gave her a conditional discharge, which meant that if she did not commit another offence within a year of that appearance in court that would be an end to the matter. For some reason I believed she had turned over a new leaf and I did not expect to see her in the courts again. It just went to prove that leopards can and do change their spots but I regret only rarely.

The only thing that was missing from her new life was a reconciliation with her father and this gave me an idea, but before I could do anything about it the police telephoned me to say that I had a client in the cells requiring my services.

The charge was shoplifting and there was no argument because the defendant had been caught on the store video, hiding a torch in her shopping bag.

"Caught red-handed," said the Custody Sergeant. "It's a shame though, she's an old lady. Her name is…….."

I interrupted him,

"Monica Jeffries?"

"How did you know that?"

"It was just a suspicion, call it a sixth sense if you like."

"Well, she was caught on video. It's so obvious. The store say she's always in there."

"Vernon's I suppose?" I asked thoughtfully.

"How on earth did you know that?" asked a surprised sergeant, "Sixth sense I suppose?"

"Yes, I suppose so. Can I come down now, you won't be keeping her will you?"

"No, I don't suppose so. We'll do a short interview and then we'll bail her to court."

The sergeant was as good as his word and a much embarrassed Monica Jeffreys went home clutching a pink charge sheet and an appointment to see me later in the week.

I never felt more pleased to see anybody prosecuted because I thought this was the opportunity I'd been waiting for to get Monica the help she needed. Ray Turton's case was adjourned again because one of the witnesses was ill and then he was extremely cross indeed to be given Christmas Eve as his trial date. I tried to avoid that date, telling the court that I was not working on Christmas Eve and did not want to come to court to do a trial. The Magistrates told me that I would have to instruct a Barrister or an agent to deal with the case, but despite my protests Christmas Eve was the date fixed for the trial.

When I went outside the court I met Turton. He was livid. "I might be looking at bastard bird 'ere and you get my case in on Christmas Eve."

"I think Ray you heard me object to Christmas Eve, because to be frank it doesn't suit me either and I'd arranged to have that day off, so don't come complaining to me. If you like I'll not bother coming in and you can represent yourself."

"It's as good as. What I need is somebody who'll fight and not be pushed around by these girkin Magistrates, anyway I'm not turning up."

"Is that a definite Ray, because if you're not turning up they'll just issue a Warrant and there's no point me turning in."

In fairness he had a point and I could well understand his annoyance, but he seemed to think that he was the only person who was inconvenienced. However I'd learned that that was the way of things and it was usually considered the solicitor's fault when the case didn't go well, so why should this be an exception?

I went back to the office but Monica didn't turn up for her appointment, which concerned me because she had always turned up in the past and had always been early. Tracey remarked upon it as well so I telephoned the house but there was no reply.   Throughout the day I tried again but there was still no answer, so I decided that I would call on my way home, but just before I set off for home I telephoned my private detective friend John Bradwell, who helped us with tricky divorce jobs or finding people who did not want to be found, to give him details of Janet Wadkin's (FiFi Dupont's) father and asked that he trace him.   If he couldn't find him, no one would.

I left the office at about six thirty and arrived at Monica's house at about quarter to seven.   She lived in a very good area of Rotherham in a detached bungalow having a very small but neat and tidy garden and as I walked up the drive there was a welcoming feel about the place.   I knocked on the door but there was no answer so noticing a bell on the wall, I rang it and had almost given up when through the smoked glass of the front door I saw a figure walking towards me.   It was Monica and she was very surprised to see me.

"Mr Smith, what on earth are you doing….. ?   Why……? What have you come for?"

"Well you didn't turn up for your appointment today Monica, and to be honest with you we were quite worried."

"Oh, I'm very sorry about that, but I haven't been feeling very well today.   I meant to ring but I just never got round to it."

There was an air of resignation about her, which I found most disquieting and I got the distinct impression that she was unhappy at receiving unwelcome visitors but that she felt obliged to invite me in.

"Well, would you like to come in for a moment?   I'm going to bed early tonight, but if you'd like to stay for just a little while……."

I had taken the hint and told her that I had to be home for seven o'clock because my tea would be on the table which seemed to placate her, so much so that she reflected upon her apparent discourtesy and her conscience forced her to insist that I stay for a cup of tea.

As we entered the very neat and tidy hallway, I inadvertently knocked a considerable amount of post from a small shelf onto the floor. So I apologised and offered to pick it all up as Monica made her way to the kitchen.

"Please go into the room," she said as she disappeared behind a solid door leading into the rear of the bungalow.

I picked up the letters to return them to the shelf and as I did so I noticed that there were two doors opposite each other in the hallway, as well as two further doors beyond and then in the centre, the door which I presumed had taken her to the kitchen. I made a choice of the door on the left and as I walked in I was shocked to find the room was being used for storage. There were shelves on the walls which housed scores of deodorants, after-shaves and similar items whilst on the floor, in open-sided boxes, was a veritable Aladdin's cave of hardware and electrical goods. For all the world it looked like a well-used storeroom and on closer scrutiny I saw that all the items which came into focus had the Vernon's Supermarket stamp on them. I quickly retired into the hallway, closing the door quietly and then entered the door on the right, which led into a most pleasant sitting-room.

I took a seat on the settee, and whilst I waited for her I looked around the room, noticing that on each available item of furniture there were photographs. Monica was featured on some of them but in the main they were of two males, one I presumed to be her husband and the other her son, pictured at various stages of his development.

On the sideboard there was a photograph of Monica, flanked at each side by her husband and son and at each side of that there were large candles which were both lit. I noticed a large album-type book on the coffee table and I couldn't resist looking into it, to discover as I flicked over a few pages that there were photographs of a baby, then a small child growing into maturity until the final page showed a man with a mortarboard and gown. There could be no doubt he was Monica's son.

I heard Monica walking along the hallway so I quickly closed up the photo album and put it back in the place I had found it, sitting back in my chair until the door opened and Monica walked in. I stood up and helped to carry the tray which held two bone china teacups with a matching teapot, sugar bowl and milk jug.

"What a lovely tea service," I said, trying to start up a conversation.

"Yes," said Monica, "It's very old; it actually belonged to my mother. I don't think you'll see one like that in existence. It's actually from Japan. My grandfather was quite a traveller in his day and he brought it back with him. Somebody once said that it was worth a lot of money."

Monica placed my cup on a coaster on the coffee table in front of me and I noticed that her hand shook as she poured the milk, then the tea, into a silver tea strainer which had been perched conveniently across my cup. She then left the room to return in an instant with a matching side plate containing some biscuits, and I felt obliged to eat two of them so as not to cause offence.

"I hope you don't mind this intrusion Monica, but we were genuinely worried about you."

Monica looked at me as though she had not quite taken in what I had said and then after a gap of some seconds she spoke.

"Oh that's all right.   In fact it's nice of you to call and so very thoughtful."

I'd noticed that the otherwise ever-present scones were significantly absent from the plate, and it seemed that for once she'd not been baking but I chose not to mention it.

"Are you ready for court tomorrow?" I asked.

Monica squinted and her face was etched with discomfort.

"I suppose I've no alternative," she said quietly.   "This is the first time I've done anything like this you see.......all the other times I was innocent, I really was.........but this time I've been very silly."

I sensed that she was in urgent need of some sympathy.

"Of course it was a silly thing to do but these things happen and in fairness you've not been well.   To be frank with you Monica I've been very worried about your health."

She stood up and walked to the front window, turning her back to me, almost hiding her face and I saw her lift her right hand in which she was holding a handkerchief.

"Come on Monica, this is something that we can face together, you're not on your own you know.   I'll be with you all the time.   You won't have to say anything other than to give your name and address and then the word 'Guilty'.   You can leave the rest to me and I promise you, you will be all right.

She turned quite dramatically and with a piercing stare as if looking for the truth in my eyes she spoke.

"Do you really think so?"

"Yes, I do.   In fact I'm so confident about it I promise you it will be all right.   The court will probably want reports from a Probation Officer and there is always the possibility............" She interrupted me,

"You mean a psychiatrist will have to see me, don't you?"

"Yes, but please don't be upset about that, there is no suggestion that ...." She interrupted me again.

"Do you really think it would be a good thing?"

I smiled in encouragement as I spoke.

"It is a good thing Monica, I'm not going to lie to you. For some time now I've felt that you are ill.   I think that you are suffering from a depressive illness but more importantly I know it can be treated and you will be well again."

She slumped into a large armchair.

"People will think that I've gone mad," she said despondently.

"No they won't," I said, "They wont think that at all, in fact who's going to know?"

"But the press will be there and they'll tell everybody."

"No they won't, your case is likely to be dealt with in the afternoon and the press don't usually come then, and if they do I'll try everything I can to persuade them not to print anything."

"So you think it won't get in the papers then?"

"No," I replied, "It won't, and in any event even if they were to be there I wouldn't let anybody refer to the report in open court."

She seemed to be appeased by what I'd said.

"I know you wouldn't let me down," she said, "But will I have to go to a mental hospital?"

240

"Of course not," I said laughing, "You will have to be assessed at first and from the information I've been given they will probably be able to do that on an out-patient basis and that will be in a psychiatrist's office."

"Have you any idea who I would see?"

"Yes, not that I'd pre-planned this or anything but I wanted some advice so I spoke to a consultant psychiatrist whom I know called Dr Gittlestone and he's a very nice man indeed. You can't help but like him, he's a gentleman."

Monica seemed soothed to some extent and seizing the opportunity, I looked at my watch.

"Have you got to get off?" she asked.

"Yes, it's tea-time and I don't want my dog to get it."

She laughed.

As I got up to leave I looked again at the photographs.

"I take it these photographs are of your husband and son?"

"Yes, they are," she said. "It's funny, I've been looking at the photograph album only this afternoon."

"Oh, really," I said.

"Yes, this is it. You can look at it if you like."

She handed me the book and I flicked through the pages.

"They all appear to be of the same person."

"Yes, it's my son Roger. It's the various stages of him growing up, right up until he passed out at university. That's the last photograph that you're looking at with him in his mortarboard and gown. I remember that day as though it was yesterday. It was one of the proudest days of my life…." Her voice tailed off into silence.

I watched her carefully as she spoke, and it was clear that she had still not come to terms with the tragedy. She continued,

"We were all very close, we had a lovely family unit, never had any problems and then they were both taken away from me."

She sat back in her chair and put her hand to her head as if concealing her eyes from view.

"They would both be very ashamed of me now," she said, almost in a whisper.

"I don't think so Monica," I said, "I think they'd be very pleased at how brave you are."

"Brave?"

"Yes, brave.   It takes a lot of doing to admit something like this."

"Thank you for being so nice," she said, "I'll do whatever you want."

"It's for the best Monica, I promise you."

"I won't go to prison will I?"

"Of course you won't, you have my word on that.   I'm so confident that if they did send you, I'd do the sentence for you."

"I suppose you'd like that, being in a woman's prison," she said smiling.

I laughed.

"Not if you saw the state of some of the women in there! I'll be off then Monica and I'll tell you what I'll do, I'll pick you up in the morning and if you don't mind waiting in my office for twenty minutes while I go through my files, I'll walk to court with you."

"Oh, that's lovely," said Monica, "Thank you very much indeed."

I walked along the hallway to the front door and I saw that inexplicably the door to the storeroom where all the stolen property was kept was slightly ajar.   Monica walked in front of me, closed it quickly then opened the front door allowing me to leave.

"There is one thing Monica," I said.

"What's that?"

"Could you bake some scones?"

"All right," she said with a smile. "I'll see what I can do."

When I got to the garden gate, I turned to look at the front door where Monica was standing and waving. She was in tears and I saw no useful purpose in staying, so I got into the car to drive away, but I could not help but think just how cruel life can be.

The following morning I was at Monica's house at fifteen minutes past eight where she was already waiting for me and she invited me in. We sat in the same front room with tea served in china cups as before but this time she had been baking and there were fresh warm scones on a small side plate on the coffee table accompanied by a matching butter dish. In those days I didn't usually eat in a morning but she had got up extra early to bake the scones especially for me, so I felt it was important that I should eat one.

Within ten minutes we were speeding our way to the office where I dropped Monica off whilst I parked the car, and she sat in the waiting room reading the paper whilst Vera made her a cup of tea as I set about reading my files.

We set off for court about nine fifteen where on arrival I took her out of the waiting area to sit in the back of the court, away from the snide Rolex watch salesmen and the purveyors of stolen cigarettes and clothing. There was one man on the corridor actively trying to sell a brand new Hoover and another with a telephone which looked as though it had been taken out of a public telephone box.

I arranged for the case to be called on first when a very timid Monica Jeffries stood in the dock and entered a guilty plea to the charge. I explained a little of the background to the Magistrates and suggested that this was a case where the court would benefit from the preparation of social enquiry reports by the Probation Service. I told the court that Monica had been observed to be suffering from depression since the death of her husband and her son, to find that fortunately the Bench were very sympathetic when they agreed to adjourn the case and order reports.

The difficulty was that the court had a very busy schedule just before Christmas and the only slot they had in the list to finish Monica's case was on Christmas Eve, but I didn't object to the adjournment because I thought if we could resolve the matter before Christmas it would be all the better for her. The only other difficulty was that Christmas Eve was the day fixed for Turton's trial, but I explained the problem to the Bench, who were kind enough to put the two cases in the same court so that I would be able to deal with them both.

I escorted Monica outside and I was talking to her when I became aware of the presence of a youth who was clearly wanting to talk to me and as I was mid-sentence Ray Turton interrupted me.

"I've been trying to find thee all day."

"If you wouldn't mind Ray I'm just in the middle of a conversation. If you'd be kind enough to wait a minute then I'll speak to you," I said.

"You'll bleeding well speak to me now, you've cocked my case up so I want it sorting out."

He would not be deterred and I turned to Monica and said,

"Monica, would you mind hanging on for me while I just deal with this. I'm sorry about the rude interruption."

She nodded, seeing the difficulty, and I turned to Turton.

"What do you mean by interrupting me like this? Have you never heard of manners?"

"Sod that old thieving cow, let's sort an important case out, like mine. I'm not turning up on Christmas Eve so you can get it adjourned. It's your cock-up that I'm in before Christmas."

"I've got nothing to do with the court list, I have no power over it. If the court order that you've got to appear on Christmas Eve, that's it. There's nothing I can do."

"You could have refused, that's what you could have done. You could have stood up and fought like you're supposed to do, instead of being a wimp."

"Ray, I'm not going to fall out with you this morning I've got too many things to do. If you're not satisfied with my services please feel free to instruct somebody else."

"Don't think you're going to get out of it like that. You've cocked up and you're going to get out of it, so you'd better get that case adjourned and it had better not be Christmas Eve," and with that he stormed off.

I turned to Monica again, "I'm sorry about that Monica, but not all my clients are as pleasant as you."

"Oh, I understand," she said, "What an ignorant man. I've seen him before in this court, you should have told him to get lost."

"It wouldn't make any difference to a man like that, but anyway you've got to be back on Christmas Eve, so if you like I'll call and pick you up again."

"That's lovely," she said, "I think I'll have a little walk round town and then I'll go home."

"Will you be all right?"

"Of course I will, I'm all right."

"Very good. Here's the Probation Officer now and I want you to have a word with her and she will explain what is going to happen."

The Probation Officer came towards us, shook hands with Monica, put her arm around her shoulder and led her away to the Probation room. I watched as they walked away together and I could not help but feel relief.

When I got back to the office John Bradwell had left me a message to say he had found Janet's (alias FiFi) father and had left his address and telephone number. I was resolved to contact him.

The next three weeks passed quickly so that by Christmas Eve the office was bedecked with trimmings and the reception featured a six foot tall Christmas tree with a number of lights. Sean Page had visited us to put a model Hitler on the top instead of a fairy which added a certain je ne sais quoi to the atmosphere.

We were closing the office at one o'clock and everyone was going to the Cross Keys for our usual Christmas Eve get-together. Wilf was in civvies and was pulling his hair out trying to complete the sale of a house for one of our clients who was waiting outside the bungalow with a furniture wagon. I drove to Monica's to collect her so that we could travel to the court together, and I had been in touch with the Probation Service who had told me that their report would recommend probation with a condition that she had out-patients psychiatric treatment. Doctor Gittlestone gave a report supporting what the Probation Officer had said so all we needed was a good Bench, full of

Christmas spirit and we would get Monica the treatment she needed.

As I walked along the court corridor I saw Turton at the end, sitting on a radiator, sneering.

"What time does tha call this?" he asked.

I looked down at my watch and shouted, "Nine twenty-five precisely."

"Clever dick," came the reply.

"I'll see you in a minute Ray, I've got something else to deal with."

"Like 'ell you 'ave, you'll get me dealt with and sod that thieving old cow!"

I had stood just about as much as I could from this loud-mouthed offensive, ignorant yob and seeing that Monica had heard what he had said, I turned to face him. I was about to let fly before my common sense took charge once again.

"I suggest you find somewhere to sit, preferably on your own, and I will come and speak to you when I have done this other case, like it or not."

Turton just shrugged his shoulders and made some comment about poor service. I took Monica into court.

Keith Copley was the Clerk that day, which meant that things would run smoothly. I asked him who was sitting on the cases, to be told to my horror that it was my 'favourite' Magistrate who I had nicknamed the 'Lord Chief Justice' and two others. The Clerk addressed Monica and she answered as politely as she could, confirming her name, address, date of birth and the fact that she pleaded guilty. She was invited to sit down by the 'Lord Chief' and the Prosecutor read out the facts briefly and handed in her record.   Before I had a chance to say anything the 'Lord Chief' interjected,

"This is a very serious record Mr Smith."

"No it isn't," I thought to myself but I wasn't going to argue.

"I've seen much worse sir but I take your point, although I would like to say that there are some very helpful reports in this case which will set out the background.   I don't propose to read the reports out but I wonder if you would be kind enough to retire and consider them?   They contain all that I wish to say and the recommendation is for a Probation Order with a condition of out-patient treatment."

The 'Lord Chief' looked surprised but he accepted the reports and the Bench retired to read them.

Turton put his head round the door, glowered at me and spoke.

"'Ow long are we going to be now?   We 'aven't been through my evidence yet."

Whilst the Magistrates had retired I decided to speak to him.

"Why don't we go into the interview room Mr Turton where we can speak in private."

"Suit yerself," said Turton and off we went to the rathole interview room at the end of the corridor.   Turton flicked his cigarette end in the direction of one of the WRVS volunteers and followed me.

I'd been told by the Prosecutor that only three of the five complainants had turned up therefore two of the three charges would have to be dropped, so I explained the position to the world's most ignorant man.

"That's not good enough," growled Turton.

"Well it's forty per cent of your charges down already," I said.

"That's no good to me, I want a hundred per cent and nothing less."

Of the three charges left, three elderly ladies were involved, all of whom I had no doubt had been duped by the wretched Turton. We went through the evidence which seemed to hinge upon whether or not the ladies were told that there might be a long delay before the work would be done. If they stuck to their evidence story which said that he'd promised to be back within the month and the court believed them, he would be found guilty.

The emphysemic usher knocked on the door and called me back into court.

"Be quick," growled Turton.

"Oh, bollocks," I said under my breath and went into court. For once the 'Lord Chief' was very sympathetic and if I may say, dealt with the sentencing exercise extremely well. He told Monica that he was saddened to see a lady of her age appear before the court but having read all the reports in the case was quite satisfied that the best thing to do was to place her on probation. Keith Copley reminded him about the requirement for out-patient treatment and he simply confirmed that that would be the case and Monica was asked if she consented. She did and with her head bowed she left the court.

I went outside to see her and she was sitting on her own on the corridor, looking quite forlorn. The Probation Officer was very pleasant and helpful, explaining to her that after the Christmas holiday the psychiatrist would contact her when she should attend the first of her appointments. She thanked the Probation Officer and then came to thank me, but just before she was able to do so Turton raised his ugly head yet again.

"Listen luv, you've 'ad your shout, now bugger off and let a man get his case done."

Monica took a pace back and with the culmination of the Turton offensive and the trauma of the hearing, she began to cry.

That was the straw that broke the camel's back. I took Monica to one side and I demanded that Turton join me in the rathole interview room. I had had enough of his bad language, his moaning, his groaning and his insults and I decided that he was going to get both barrels.

"You are the crudest, most offensive, ignorant man I've ever met! You have a foul mouth, you're dishonest and more importantly you are a heartless bully! Of all the clients I have met in my long career, I have never met anyone as unpleasant as you! I have considered the evidence very carefully in your case and the Prosecutor is withdrawing two of the charges against you. The other three charges involve three ladies, one of whom is in a wheelchair and has been brought here to give evidence against you. All three of them are extremely concerned at having to give evidence but from what I have been told, one in particular is so adamant as to what you said and did, that I have absolutely no doubt that the Magistrates will believe her. Furthermore, when you give your evidence, not only will you come over badly but the impression you will give to the court will be of a thoroughly despicable and unpleasant git! In those circumstances you either plead Guilty to the three remaining charges or you walk in that court and represent yourself because I am sick and tired of having to put up with you and your behaviour, and in addition, when you address me in future you call me Mr and you do not speak to me when I am speaking to someone else. Also, do not interrupt an old lady when she is speaking because if you do I'm afraid I am likely to kick you right up the jacksie. Do I make myself clear?"

Turton's mouth dropped wide open and he just stared and looked at me as though in a state of shock.

"So, it's guilty pleas to all three isn't it?" I asked firmly.

Turton didn't reply and simply nodded. He followed me into court where with various promptings he entered guilty pleas to the charges.

I thought I did a fairly good job in mitigation, having addressed the court at some length. I suppose it was a kind of payback, having abused Turton so forcefully only minutes before, I felt obliged to do my very best for him. I must have done extremely well because the court took the unusual step of giving him a suspended sentence which meant that he would not have to go to prison unless he re-offended. He had secured his Christmas at liberty, although quite who would have wanted him as a dinner guest was beyond me. He walked out of court without saying a word, but I didn't expect any thanks from the likes of him.

When I went out into the court corridor Monica was waiting for me and I thought that she'd aged quite substantially over the past few weeks because somehow her steps now seemed to falter a little.

We called at the office where all the staff were busy pouring out drinks for the lunchtime toast, and Monica had a glass of sherry so I got everyone to toast her future health and happiness and she seemed quite pleased.

The mood changed when in walked Ray Turton. The whole room went quiet.

"What can I do for you now?" I asked sarcastically.

"You may as well have this for your trouble," said Ray putting a bottle of malt whisky on the counter, "I don't want anybody to say that I'm a mean bastard. I've not nicked it, the receipt's in the bag to prove it. So there!"

As he was leaving he turned and spoke again.

"Anyway," he said thoughtfully.

"Yes?" I responded.

"Well...... I'm going, I've better things to do than being sat in 'ere watching you lot enjoying yourselves."

With that he left the office and closed the door.

"I suppose that meant 'thank you'," said Wilf.

"I suppose it did."

Just then FiFi, or should I say Janet Wadkin came into the reception. She was carrying a bottle of gin and a card.

"Thank you for my invitation," she said, "I can only stay a short time because it's the party at the Home this afternoon and I don't want to be late."

"OK, pull up a chair and get yourself a drink."

"Could I be boring and have a tea, I've packed in booze?"

"Oh, I'm impressed, but tea it is, now sit down."

She had brought her boss with her who told me that Janet had talked him into putting some work our way preparing Wills, which was a very good contact. Janet herself was very good in company and we were impressed with how she had changed both in dress and attitude.

Just then Tracey told me that another guest had arrived and was asking for me in reception, so I went into the main waiting area where there was a grey-haired man of about sixty-five who walked with a slight stoop and the aid of a silver-topped walking stick.   He was breathless and sat on a chair to rest.

"Is she really here Mr Smith?" he asked.

"Yes, she is.   I presume you are Mr Wadkin, but she doesn't know you are here."

"Goodness me, its years since I've seen her.   I wonder what she'll say when she sees me?"

"I think she'll be delighted.   She's here with her boss."

"Her boss?"

"Yes, she's doing very well as a care assistant, looking after the elderly and in fact she's going on a course soon as she intends to get some qualifications."

Mr Wadkin was delighted.   I gave him a drink and made my way into the main office in search of his daughter.   I interrupted her conversation with one of our other clients and suggested that she might like to meet a rather interesting gentleman who was sitting in the waiting room. Intrigued she put down her drink and walked with me.

"After you," I said and directed her into the waiting room. Her eyes lit up as she came upon the familiar face in the corner.   Mr Wadkin struggled to his feet and they embraced.

I could not help but smile as I closed the door but I thought they would prefer to be alone.

I was talking to my friend Tim Johnson, the manager of the Bradford & Bingley Building Society, when a face appeared at the door.

It was a grinning face with a preponderance of gum and a bright cheeky smile staring directly at me.   There was only one person in the world that could be.   It was of course Albert Heptonstall and he was holding a fist full of pink sheets. Albert continued to grin as he thrust the charge sheets into my hand.

"Now then, Mr Smith, just when you thought it was safe to come out of the water, 'ere I am," he said, continuing to grin.

I looked at the charge sheets to find that they related to someone called Michael Seafield.

"But these aren't your charges Albert."

"Of course they're not," said Albert looking at me, "I wouldn't do such a thing would I?"

The thought then occurred to me that Albert had given a false name to the police. My years of dealing with criminal work had made me cynical and had prompted me to imagine the worst possible scenario. Albert had lied to the police and given them a false name, was even now perverting the course of justice and I was being dragged into the conspiracy!

Before I could blurt out my annoyance, Albert started to laugh.

"They're not for me Steve, they're from someone in our street who 'as never been in trouble before and wanted me to recommend a solicitor, so I've told 'im to see you."

I soon discounted my conspiracy theory with a sigh of relief.

"Caroline met Michael at the Animal Sanctuary and 'e told 'er of 'is problems, so she spoke to me and together we 'ave recommended you," he said proudly.

"That's very good of you Albert. I'll send him an appointment."

"If you would, but I'd like to see you if I can, about something personal."

"Yes, of course," I replied and I took him into an interview room not far from reception.

I had long since ceased to shake hands with Albert because one of his party tricks was to press a handful of well-chewed bubble gum into the palm of his hand and pass it on with a hand-shake. So when he offered his hand I opened it up to see if it concealed any offensive material. Albert laughed out loud, shouted 'Gotcha' and opened his other hand to display a palmful of odious-looking material.

"Gotcha – it's in the other 'and!"

I shook my head and sat down behind my desk.

"Now then Albert, what can I do for you?"

"It's a couple of things," said Albert. "The first is that lad Michael Seafield.

"'e won't go down will 'e Steve?"

"I don't think so Albert but there are a lot of offences and the court might think a short sharp shock might be the order of the day."

"Ay, I've 'ad a few of them short sharp shocks," said Albert.

"Yes, you certainly have but it didn't work with you did it?"

"It did really. I'm clean now Steve, I've done nowt this year."

"Come to think of it Albert, that's true. What's caused this transformation?"

"What's a transformation?"

"This change, this different attitude, this new you."

"That's the other thing I wanted to talk to you about," said Albert, "It's not really business like, but I don't know 'ow to go on and me dad's no idea, in fact if 'e knew 'e'd blow 'is stack."

255

"How is Jack, I haven't seen him for a while?"

"'e's right bad with the piles," said Albert. "'e has to sit on a tyre now so that nothing comes into contact with 'is arse."

I couldn't imagine that anything would want to come into contact with Jack's arse, but I understood what he meant and our conversation continued.

"How can I help then Albert?"

Albert took a deep breath and with some reluctance he started his story.

"Well, you know I'm working at the Animal Sanctuary now?"

"Yes I do and that's very commendable."

"Ay well, I've done right well and they want it to turn into a proper job, so they've set me on proper like and I'm on the books now and no longer a violin player." (This was a slang term for being on the fiddle).

Albert paused for a little as if finding a way of explaining his problem.

"Well that Caroline bird goes, dunt she?"

"Yes," I replied, inviting Albert to get to the point.

"Well, we've become friends like, do you know what I mean?"

The realisation of what was going on just struck me.

"Well, well, well, Albert's got a girlfriend," I said.

"Don't you start, I've 'ad all that from me mum and dad and me brothers."

"I'm sorry Albert, I didn't mean to be unkind, it's just that I never had you down for being the marrying type."

"Marrying?"

Albert was most put out and I began to laugh. When he realised I was only joking he laughed too, but then returned to his story.

"No gi'o'er, it's like this. She's alreight and we work at the Sanctuary together. I've started to get a bit of wages and so I've been taking 'er out, 'ere there and everywhere."

"Really, where do you go Albert?" I asked, expressing interest.

"Pictures mainly, she likes pictures. Then she took me to the Civic last week."

"Do you mean the theatre?

"Ay, I do."

"What did you go to see?"

"Summat called Midsummer's Dream or summat."

"You mean Midsummer Night's Dream?"

"Well it were more like a bloody nightmare," said Albert, "They were talking bollocks and I couldn't understand a word of it; I pray thee this and I pray thee that....I was praying that it would bleeding end. When curtain shut after the first 'our I got up to go, I thought that were it. I didn't realise I 'ad to sit through another 'our and 'alf of the bloody shite, and the gear they were wearing; I'll tell you what, there were one bloke with a pair of white tights on and his bollocks were almost 'anging out. It were disgusting really, walking about looking like that and I think 'e were a shirt-lifter an' all."

"So I take it you don't like Shakespeare Albert?"

"I don't understand it, but even if I did I wouldn't like it."

"So how would you describe it in one word Albert?"

Albert thought for a minute.

"Crap," said Albert, "Plain, unadulterated crap. I've 'ad more fun 'aving me teeth out."

"Anyway," he continued, "We've been to other things and then she took me to one of them Chinese restaurant places."

"Oh, was it for a Cantonese meal?

"No, it were a Chinese dinner, tha knows, with them pieces of wood that you're supposed to eat thee snap with. What a farce that was! I can't see the point of 'aving two bits of wood to eat thee dinner, so I asked them for a fork and they looked at me as though I'd crawled out of our lav top. Anyway, there were no taters or chips and they'd never 'eard of burgers or fish fingers. I 'ad what tasted like a piece of cardboard for me pudding, that were crap an' all. We came out and I got a burger from that caravan at end of our street. It were a right job."

I realised that Albert's introduction to one of the world's great cuisine's had not met with great approval. I also realised that his indoctrination into the finer things of life was going to take some time.

"Not only that, I couldn't understand a word 'e said. What's the point of living 'ere if they can't speak English. I couldn't understand 'im and 'e couldn't understand me."

I couldn't help thinking there were times when I couldn't understand Albert either and I'm not Chinese, so what chance had they got?

"Then I took 'er to the dog racing and she liked that, so now we go three times a week, 'cos she likes animals."

"So you're getting on very well?"

"Ay, she's alreight, she's been 'elping me to read though and you know I'm a bit embarrassed about that but she's bin reight good and I'm definitely getting better."

"Well done Albert," I said, noting for the first time that he was actually spotlessly clean, something which I had never seen before.   There was no doubt Albert was making a substantial effort and there could only be one reason for that.   Albert appeared to have fallen in love.

"Well I understand all about Shakespeare and the meals out etc, but what exactly is the problem?"

"'E's a bloody cop!!"

"Who is?"

"Well, it's like this.   Caroline wants me to go to their 'ouse."

"Oh, I see," I said as I stood up and wandered over to the window, knowing what was coming.

"And you're a little worried about how to go on, is that it?"

"No," said Albert, "I'm not worried about that."

"Then what's the problem?"

"Well me father will go mad if 'e knows I'm going out wi' a copper's daughter and the other thing, what's the copper gunna think about me?   I suppose 'e'll check me out and find out I've got some form and then 'e'll warn 'er off."

"Does Caroline know that you had some problems when you were younger?"

"Ay, I've told 'er, to try to put 'er off, 'cos I didn't think she'd want to know me if she found out about that, but she seemed right impressed that I'd packed it in."

"And have you packed it in Albert?"

"Yes, of course I 'ave," said Albert.   "I love this job, it's great and I want to keep doing it.   If I get into bother they won't want me there."

There could be no doubt in my view that Albert was telling the truth.   It was a very odd mix, on the one hand there was Albert, not gifted with good looks or an affluent background and on the other an extremely attractive girl from a police family.   What greater contrast could there

259

be?   Caroline's family on the side of law and order and Albert's on something else.

"How do you feel about Caroline, Albert?"

"She's alreight."

"No, I mean, what do you really think?"

Albert paused for a little and seemed to be rather embarrassed.

"I think she's very much alreight," he said.

"I understand Albert, I don't wish to cause you embarrassment, but you are pretty keen aren't you?"

"Yes, I am," said Albert.   "Tell me what I've got to do.   I don't want to go but she's pushing it and 'er dad wants to meet me."

"I bet he does," I said.   "Well, why don't you get your best suit on and just be yourself."

"I 'aven't got a suit..........but I've got a Ricardo Monchetti jacket."

"No, I wouldn't bother."

I thought for a minute and then wondered if that was good advice.

"Well, when I say be yourself I mean be respectful but try not to put on any airs and graces."

"What do you mean, airs and graces?"

"I'll tell you what, just be you and I suggest that you talk about your job and work at the Animal Sanctuary and if you keep on about that you will bore them to death and keep them off other subjects."

"Shall I tell 'im I've got form?"

"No, not unless he asks, but I suggest if he does ask you should tell him the truth.   For all we know he may have checked anyway."

"Bloody 'ell," said Albert.

260

"Bloody 'ell indeed," I replied.

"Would 'e go as far as doing that?

"Well, he's a policeman isn't he and with all due respect to them, that's how they think.   They are paid to be suspicious."

"They are paid to be twats," said Albert.

"Yes I suppose so, but you mustn't tell him that."

Albert was sitting deep in thought so I interrupted him.

"You know Albert, when he finds out, and find out he will, then he's going to think a lot more of you if you're up front and honest."

"I'm embarrassed to talk about it," said Albert.

"Yes, I appreciate that, but believe me in this particular case I'm convinced that honesty is the best policy."

"Do you think 'e'll appreciate that?"

"Not particularly, but at least he'll respect your honesty and on the basis that you're going straight the best example of that is to be honest about your past."

"Bloody 'ell," said Albert.

"Bloody 'ell," I said in agreement.

I can't tell him about pinching that chemical toilet can I?"

"Only if he asks."

"Bloody 'ell," said Albert.

"Bloody 'ell," I said again in agreement.   "Well, what do you think then, Albert?"

"I think I'm not bloody goin'."

"But what if Caroline insists?"

"Then I'll go and get it over with, but I don't think they'll like me."

"I wouldn't be too sure about that Albert.   Caroline likes you."

"Yea, but she ain't a copper."

"Well, just be respectful, don't swear and don't break wind."

Albert laughed.

"Yer a rightun thee Steve, but at least tha straight."

There was no greater compliment and with that Albert said he would think about his dilemma and let me know how he went on.

"OK then Steve I'll be off, but there is one other thing…"

"Yes?"

"What do I tell me father?"

I thought for a moment.

"Well Albert, you know I advised you that honesty was the best policy?"

"Yes," replied a concerned Albert.

"Well, I suggest on this occasion you lie."

"Aye," said a relieved Albert, smiling.

"Anyway I'm off. 'Ere's your card."

Albert gave me a Christmas card.

We shook hands and I grimaced as my hand came into contact with a lump of well-chewed bubble gum. He laughed and winked, and as he left Vera George, our new cleaner, knocked on the door and walked in. She was so excited that she couldn't speak.

"What is it Mrs George, what's the matter?"

"Oh, Mr Smith," she said, "You'll never guess, oh it's wonderful, you'll never guess.

"What is it? Sit down and tell me what's gone on."

"It's my sister."

It was fairly clear that she could not conceal her delight.

"They've done all the tests and they say that they have caught it all. She's tested clear Mr Smith, she's going to be OK."

I put my arm around her shoulders and she began to cry. We were both delighted with the news and I phoned Wilford and told him. It was only a matter of a minute or so before members of staff came into the room and expressed their delight at the news.

"It looks like she'll be out for Christmas, but only for the day."

"Oh, brilliant," I said, "That will be fantastic."

"She's groggy of course and she hasn't got to do any work, but we'll look after her, we'll see to that. It'll be worth it just to have her at home."

"Well I'll tell you what Mrs George, why don't you leave the cleaning for today and you get off and go and see her."

"No it's all right, I can't get in for visiting just yet, the doctor will be seeing her at dinnertime, so I'll finish up and go this afternoon."

"All right, well when you do give her our very best wishes. I'll get Tracey to get some flowers this morning, if you could drop them in for her we would be grateful."

"I'll do that with pleasure," she said, "Isn't it wonderful!"

I nodded and smiled. How nice it was to have some good news, especially at Christmas.

There was of course the problem with the roof and the boiler wasn't working, also the typewriters needed to be changed for new ones. Then of course the company cars were three years old and needed replacing and then there was the VAT man to settle. I shuddered, thinking of the list of problems that I had to face in the New Year.

Chapter Fifteen

We Wish You A Merry Christmas, Whether Lonely or Not

The Christmas Eve session at the Cross Keys was always a grand affair with free sandwiches and pork pie for the regulars and the atmosphere was vibrant.   All the gang were there, the great Jarvis, the mad Scotsman, Bader and Goody had popped in on his way home.   Pagey was they're wearing his grandfather's First World War catering corps medal and the there was Wilf, Bodger, Lovell, Eastwood, Tim Johnson and Fred from the Eagle Star bringing up the rear.   Dave 'Over the' Hill had travelled in from Sheffield and it was a most brilliant gathering, which was subject to the usual practical jokes and childish behaviour with a plastic string and the crazy foam.   I suppose it was some kind of release of nervous tension, after a reasonably good year but one which had brought the responsibilities of employerdom.   We had grown to a staff of fifteen or sixteen people and were moving headlong into the recession which was to hit the 1980's with a vengeance.   Nevertheless, the accountant and the bank manager were reasonably happy with the figures, and we were about to enter our eighth year in practice.

As we nibbled at the black pudding which bedecked the old oak bar, music blared out from two overworked speakers which hung from the pelmet hanging precariously above the optics.   Everyone was in extremely good spirits but I could not help but think about Monica Jeffries.

She had told me that she was having a Christmas lunch with her neighbour, so at least she had some company but I was concerned about her mental state because although it was true that we had managed to set up the probation order with a condition of treatment, it would be January before that started and in addition I had found out that her son had been killed in the accident during the Christmas holidays some years before so it would be a poignant and perhaps painful anniversary.

I was also worried about her own realisation that she was ill since prior to this she had lived in a strange 'never-never land' which had led an otherwise innocent and honest woman into theft but now that her days of shoplifting were over I wondered what this appointment with reality would bring.

I was brought out of my melancholy mood by the playing of 1960's songs from a cassette the landlord had kept over the years, adding to what was a wonderful afternoon and I was glad that I'd not travelled to work in my car.

I wandered down to the taxi rank when the event was finished, just as it started to rain, and the tannoy from the church was blaring out carols, whilst passers-by and last minute shoppers were scurrying around the town as though their very lives depended upon it, dashing in and out of shops who were anxious to close. Everyone was being pleasant to everybody else and I wondered what it would really be like if people behaved like that the whole year round.

The taxi drove past the office and I could see Vera through the window, clearing up the debris from the office get-together. It had certainly been a most interesting day.

265

On the way home I travelled near Monica's house so I asked the driver to make a slight detour and whether it was my mood of melancholy or perhaps a drink too many I didn't know, but I thought I would just pop in to leave a Christmas card which I had spare in my briefcase. The lights were off and there was no one in and I thought that perhaps she might be at her friend's house next door where I'd believed she was going to spend Christmas Day.

I don't know what possessed me to do it but I decided to knock on the neighbour's door. And then I noticed their milk bottle on the step, but more significantly I could clearly see the writing on the paper inside which told the milkman that nothing was required to cover the Christmas period. I realised then that Monica would be alone at Christmas.

There had been a tradition on Christmas Eve night that I would go out for dinner with my family and close friends and this year was to be no exception. In the event we went to my friend Vito's place at Crookes in Sheffield, where we enjoyed a fine Italian meal and a good time was had by all, although I later experienced troubled sleep before getting up on Christmas morning about 9am. I decided to have an easy day, wearing my new slippers and jumper. I watched the John Wayne film on television and the traditional smattering of Christmas shows because our Christmas dinner was to be served late; no one wanted anything much to eat or drink because of the night before.

It was cold and overcast with a slight mist on the hills and I was sitting in my lounge with the Radio Times looking to see if the film *'The Guns of Navarone'* was being shown as I sipped from a glass of Alka Seltzer.

The night before had truly been a splendid event with my family and friends, but then Christmas Eve was always special, inspired by a tradition which had been going on some twenty years and continues to this day - the highlight of the Christmas period.   Christmas Day tended to be something of a damp squib by contrast, and usually took the form of a fried breakfast, the early morning film, trying out the perennial gift of a pair of slippers and starting to read a number of new books which had been carefully packaged in Christmas paper and ribbon.   My pile of presents were stacked at the side of my chair, as I flicked through each of the volumes in anticipation of spending the Christmas holiday lying on the settee, doing absolutely nothing and dividing my time between old television films and a new book: The History of Boxing Part 1.

It was an age when my daughter no longer believed in Father Christmas, and for that matter neither did I but my parents and in-laws would always arrive before the Queen's speech to help with the preparation of the main meal as well as to see what presents were coming their way.

I was watching the Bing Crosby film, 'White Christmas' for the eleventh time when my mind wandered back to thoughts of Monica Jeffries. I don't know what caused me to think of her, but it may have been the arrival of my close-knit family, which compelled me to think hard about what it must be like to be alone at Christmas, and it's odd how conversations come back to you as your mind works overtime, putting all those recollections together.   And then I thought about the milk bottle and the fact that Monica's friend was away for Christmas which meant she must be entirely alone. Whilst she had just been placed on probation and had been given the considerable assistance of Dr Gittlestone, her therapy would not start until January and understandably on Christmas Day, the Probation Service office was closed.

Then I remembered the tragic anniversary, for her son had been killed at Christmas, so what an awful time it would be for her. On the other hand, perhaps she might prefer to be alone, but then again she didn't really have any option.

I considered the circumstances for the whole of the latter part of *'White Christmas'* and it wasn't until a rather loud children's cartoon started that I was brought to my senses, when declining a bottle of beer I drank an orange juice instead. I looked at the clock which showed 11am, checked on the time of the dinner, which had been fixed for 3pm, and having made my excuses, went to my car to drive towards Rotherham.

There was still plenty of traffic about with people travelling to family parties and get-togethers but I knew that there must be some desperately lonely people, and never more so than at Christmas.

As I got to Monica's street, I had second thoughts. Perhaps she would think that I'd lost my marbles completely by turning up unannounced, especially on Christmas Day, or perhaps she would have some friends in the house and I would be an unwelcome guest. But then it was Christmas Day, I could surely make an excuse of being in the area and be simply calling in just to say hello.

I walked up the short path leading to the garden gate and I could see a light coming from the front room, so I knocked on the door but obtained no answer. I couldn't explain it but I immediately felt uncomfortable as though something was amiss, particularly when no one came to the door.

I walked to the front window, looked inside and to my horror, saw Monica slumped in an armchair. On the coffee table at the side of her was an overturned plastic bottle of pills.

Chapter Sixteen

Happy New Year?

My heart was racing and in my panic I tried the front door, which was open, so I ran inside to the lounge and shouted her name but it was never more apparent to me that I should have been our firm's first aid representative; I had absolutely no idea what to do.

My shouts seemed to disturb her and then slowly but surely she opened her eyes to find me standing over her shouting her name.

She blinked repeatedly and then spoke.

"Mr Smith, what on earth.......what on earth are you doing here, what's the matter?"

I looked at her and I looked down at the plastic bottle and saw the words 'vitamin C' emblazoned across the rim. A feeling of deep embarrassment overcame me and I stammered a rather pathetic excuse so as to conceal my feelings

"I looked in the window......I thought you weren't well........I knocked on the door but it just opened........I came inside and ...."

Thankfully Monica reassured me and in her drowsiness had simply accepted what I had said.

"What on earth are you doing here on Christmas Day?"

"Well, I was in the area and I was passing through so I thought I'd just pop in to say hello and cadge a cup of tea."

"Well I never," she said, "Fancy seeing you on Christmas Day, I can't believe it."

I then noticed a half-eaten sandwich on a plate at the other side of the chair and she caught me looking at it.

"I've just had a sandwich," she said. "My friend has gone to her son's for the day and so I'm staying in and resting."

"I thought you were at your friends for your Christmas dinner?"

"No, she's coming home tonight so we're going to have our dinner then."

I thought Monica was not being over generous with the truth.

"Would you like a cup of tea and a piece of cake?"

"Most definitely," I said, and off she went to the kitchen.

I looked around the room which was in its usual pristine condition and was struck by the total absence of Christmas cards.

Monica returned with a plate full of cakes and scones on a tray, which included neatly set out utensils and a butter dish. I ate a scone and then a piece of cake and as I finished my tea she brought in a bottle of Harveys Bristol Cream sherry, her favourite tipple. We drank the sherry together in a toast to the future and I couldn't help wondering what was in store for her.

She talked about old times and family Christmases past until it was time for me to leave.

"You're more than welcome to come back with me Monica and have Christmas dinner at my house if you wish."

"That's very kind of you," she said, "But I really couldn't eat two Christmas dinners, and not only that, everything seems to have caught up with me and I'm very tired. I don't want to be an old sourpuss but I really do need to get to bed early. Don't worry, I'll be fine after Christmas."

"Are you sure?" I asked.

"Yes, I'm sure," she said with a sigh, "Now, if you don't mind, I'm going to prepare a little bit of dinner for me and my friend."

"Of course," I said, helping her to keep up the pretence.

"Look, I'll call in to see you just after the Christmas holidays, or come down to the office if you like, we'd all be pleased to see you."

"Yes, I'll do that," she said, "I'll call in before New Year and bring some buns and scones."

"Yes, you better had, so I suggest you have a big baking session one day and then we'll eat them all – it'll be like feeding the five thousand!"

She laughed and I think she was glad of the opportunity to do something for someone else.

I finished my glass of sherry and moved to the door.

"Thank you very much for coming," said Monica.

"It was a pleasure," I said, "And after all I was passing through this area."

"Of course you were," she said, although I suspected she hadn't believed a word of what I was saying.

Monica stood at the door and waved to me while I walked to the car. We were just beginning to lose the day's light and the chill in the air made me shudder. She waved again and closed the door as I drove away, leaving her alone with her thoughts and her memories. I'd done the best I could but it wasn't really enough.

When I arrived home the dinner was just about ready, but having eaten two scones and three pieces of cake I wasn't really hungry.

Rebecca, my daughter, had a number of presents including one of those games which requires a terrific amount of thought and input to participate. After dinner I lost three of the games before falling asleep in the chair.

When I awoke I found myself reviewing the events of the past year in my mind. There was the argument with the taxman and the bank, which upset me at the time and took me so long to get over.

Then of course there was the unfortunate and untimely death of Michael Wellington McIver, otherwise known as Spider; how futile it seemed that someone so young should die from being involved in such a filthy trade.

There was Mrs Mott and her illness which gave rise to the advent of her 'stand-in' the remarkable Vera, who took pleasure in forcing her peculiar herbal mixtures down my throat as though I was some recalcitrant schoolboy.

There were the football matches and the monthly soirées with my boozing pals, and of course the success story of FiFi DuPont who was so happily reconciled with her proud and delighted father.

There was also Monica, whose life had effectively ended that fateful Christmas when her son was killed in the crash. I could see her sitting in her front room alone, with only her photographs and her memories for company. Justice, comedy and tragedy had written the history of our year gone by.

We were now looking at a great venture for 1989, a new office with plenty of room and a prestigious address at 22 Westgate, Rotherham. All in all, it hadn't been too bad a year.

It was the custody sergeant at Rotherham police station whose duty decreed that he disturbed me on Christmas Day evening, and I trudged reluctantly to the telephone to answer it.

"Good evening Mr Smith," said Sergeant Webster, "I'm sorry to disturb you on Christmas Day, but we have two prisoners in the cells and one of them is asking for you."

"Two prisoners?" I asked.

"Yes," said the sergeant, "One I'm not troubling you with because he hasn't asked for you but the other has. Yours is a young man called Albert Heptonstall, do you know him?"

"Oh, I know him all right," I said, "What's he done?"

"Well," said the sergeant, "He was arrested this morning at his home. He was seen to be fitting Christmas lights around his front door."

"That's not an offence," I replied impatiently.

"It is if the lights are off the Town Hall Christmas tree!"

"Oh," I replied somewhat deflated.

"I'll bring him to the phone, just hang on a minute."

"Most certainly sergeant, I will. By the way, as a matter of interest, what's the other done?"

"Oh, it's something to do with a drug death. A young kid with an unusual name took an overdose earlier this year and we think that this lad supplied him with the drugs. It seems as though he's going to admit it as well, so whether they're going to charge him with manslaughter or not we don't know yet. Anyway, I'll fetch the other lad to the 'phone, if you'd be kind enough to have a word with him sir." said the sergeant, laughing into the 'phone, "Oh, and I'm sorry to disturb your Christmas Day celebrations whilst I am at work."

"Yes, I suppose I'll have a word with him," I said with a sigh, after all he was my 'favourite' client.

"Before you do, what did they call the lad with the unusual name?"

274

"Let me look," said the sergeant, "I've got the papers here. Yes, here it is; Michael Wellington McIver. Why do you ask, did you know him?"

I sat down on the chair at the side of the telephone table.

"Yes," I said with a sigh, "I knew him. He was a client of mine.

"Oh, not any more Mr Smith," he replied with heavy irony.

"Yes....you're right....not any more," I said thoughtfully.

Just then a familiar voice spoke,

"Is that Steve Smith?"

"Yes, it's me and may I say Merry Christmas to you Albert."

"Ay. Listen..."

"I am listening."

"These coppers 'ave got me locked up 'ere in the police station."

I resisted the temptation to say, "Oh, really? I thought you were phoning from the British Embassy in Guatemala," but then I realised just how upset Albert would be in being away from his family on Christmas Day. I also remembered that I was a solicitor who had taken the Hippocratic Oath not to whinge and whine when he was interrupted or inconvenienced on his days off by clients who, in the main, really didn't deserve it.

Then I also remembered that Albert's family were my best clients and after all he did buy me a watch which I threw away in the River Don because I thought he'd pinched it.

Pricked by my conscience I decided the only proper thing to do was to help him as best I could.

"Well Albert, you'd best tell me all about it."

Albert took a deep breath and began.

"Well," he said, "You know me..."

275

"Yes, I do," I replied, "I most certainly do."
"Well," said Albert, "You'll never believe this ….."
"And do you know, he was right!"
TO BE CONTINUED…….

Neville-Douglas Publishing Ltd
present

Boozers
Ballcocks
&
Bail

by
Stephen D Smith

Boozers Ballcocks & Bail is a no-holds-barred account of
the life of a thriving criminal law practice in an industrial
northern town in the early eighties. It opens the door on
the law in a totally honest and compelling way, giving an
insight into the sometimes tragic, but often hilarious world
of law courts, prison cells and solicitors' offices.
"….Laugh out loud material," - BBC
"….Steve Smith is the legal James Herriot," – Yorkshire Post

Pages: 256   Size: 216x138   ISBN: 1-871647-33-9
Price: £8.99 including postage & packing from:

Neville-Douglas Publishing Ltd
Clumber Lodge, Hemingfield Road,
Wombwell, Barnsley, Yorkshire S73 OLY
Tel: 01226 753324   Fax: 01226 758462

Neville-Douglas Publishing Ltd

present

Plonkers
Plaintiffs
&
Pleas

by
Stephen D Smith

Plonkers Plaintiffs & Pleas is the sequel to the hilarious Boozers Ballcocks & Bail which was the first book in the comedy series relating what it is really like behind the closed doors of the legal profession. **Plonkers Plaintiffs & Pleas** continues the story with page after page of laugh out loud material.

"...Brilliantly funny book." – Charlie Williams

"...A hilarious book." – Yorkshire Television

Pages: 256   Size: 216x135   ISBN: 1-901853-10-1
Price: £8.99 including postage & packing from:

Neville-Douglas Publishing Ltd
Clumber Lodge, Hemingfield Road,
Wombwell, Barnsley, Yorkshire S73 OLY
Tel: 01226 753324   Fax: 01226 758462

Neville-Douglas Publishing Ltd
present the book that was banned

HELL IS NOT FOR ANGELS

by Stephen D Smith

Subject of two BBC Rough Justice Programmes

On 13 July 1990 John Megson was convicted of murder at Leeds Crown Curt. The Judge gave him the mandatory life sentence and recommended that he serve no less than 15 years! John Megson was an innocent man and it was to take five years for justice to be done.

In April 1989, a camper was fatally stabbed after upsetting members of Megson's motorcycle gang, the Druids. Megson alone was convicted of the killing and because he refused to break the bikers' code of silence he went to prison for a crime he did not commit. For two years John's father tried to persuade him to name the real killer. He knew his son was innocent. He then contacted Steve Smith.

A single meeting with John in Wakefield Prison convinced a solicitor with 26 years in the legal profession that an innocent man was serving a life sentence for a murder he had not committed. He realised that "I was stuck with John Megson and he with me whether we liked it or not."

Pages: 264   Size: 216x138   ISBN: 1-901853-00-4
Price: £8.99 including postage & packing from:

Neville-Douglas Publishing Ltd
Clumber Lodge, Hemingfield Road,
Wombwell, Barnsley, Yorkshire S73 OLY
Tel: 01226 753324   Fax: 01226 758462

Neville-Douglas Publishing Ltd

present

'CHARLIE' THE CHARLIE WILLIAMS STORY

by
Stephen D Smith

SOLD OUT

The authorised biography of the great black comedian Charlie Williams, charting his life from schooldays to professional football and then as a great star of showbusiness.

contributions from many including, Bobby Knutt, Duggie Brown, Roy Walker, Gary Wilmot, Joe Longthorne, Vince Hill, Norman Collier and Sir David Frost.

Pages: Size: 216x135 **ISBN: 1 901853 50 0**

Neville-Douglas Publishing Ltd
Clumber Lodge, Hemingfield Road,
Wombwell, Barnsley, Yorkshire S73 OLY
Tel: 01226 753324 Fax: 01226 758462

Neville-Douglas Publishing Ltd
present

SHOEBOX TO SILVER SHOES

by
Stephen D Smith

The remarkable story of Trisha, the Medium, telling of her life from the moment she was left as a new-born baby in a shoebox on convent steps, to her adoption into a Chinese family.

Following her adoptive father's tragic death she ended up as a child prostitute on the streets of Kowloon, but then she was visited by spirit and her enlightenment began.

The story follows her life from an involvement in murder to her return to England and eventually, the ability to speak with people from the past.

Pages: 192   Size: 216x135   ISBN: 1 902853 51 9
Price: £8.99 including postage & packing from:

Neville-Douglas Publishing Ltd
Clumber Lodge, Hemingfield Road,
Wombwell, Barnsley, Yorkshire S73 OLY
Tel: 01226 753324   Fax: 01226 758462